# Through The Glass Ceiling

## Honor Moore Muller
*as told to*
## Charles Franklin Hutchins

**PARK PLACE PUBLICATIONS**
Pacific Grove, California

Through The Glass Ceiling
Honor Moore Muller
*as told to* Charles Franklin Hutchins
Copyright © 2019 Charles Franklin Hutchins/Honor Moore Muller
ISBN 978-1-943887-99-6

First Edition March 2016
Second Edition February 2020
All rights reserved, except as permitted under the U.S. Copyright Act of 1976, no part of this publication may be reproduced, distributed or transmitted in any form or by any means, or stored in a data base or retrieval system, without the prior written permission of the author.

"The Glass Ceiling" is a metaphor used to represent an invisible barrier that keeps a demographic (typically applied to minorities) from rising beyond a certain level in the hierarchy. The metaphor was first coined by feminists about barriers to high-achieving women in the U.S.

The Glass Ceiling Commission, and its definition, was created by Congress as part of Title II of the Civil Rights Act of 1991. The definition says that although those affected can see the position they seek, it cannot be reached because of discrimination. It was created to diversify the business world. —*Jim Tunney, The Monterey County Herald*

# Dedication

*To all the people in my life who contributed to my career from the first rung in the climb up the ladder of success, from humble beginnings in Hudson, New York, becoming an elected corporate officer of a major corporaton, "Through the Glass Ceiling" to self-sufficiency, good health and happiness.*

*To the memory of my husband of 35 years, Leonard (Len) Frederick Muller.*

*To the memory of my parents, Mahlon Horatio Moore and Henrietta Dohrmann Moore.*

*To the memory of my four brothers; Claude Richard Moore, Aubrey Mahlon Moore, Mahlon (Mally) Horatio Moore Jr. and Milton (Milt) George Moore and my two sisters; Lillian (Lil) Anita Moore and Margaret (Mickey) Lois Moore.*

*— And especially to my devoted and loving friend, Charles Franklin Hutchins, whose encouragement made this book possible.*

*Honor Moore Muller**
*Carmel, CA 2019*

\* *Honor speaking will appear in italics throughout the book.*

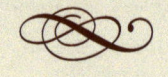

# Prologue

This is the story of a small town daughter's rise out of the depression era to be elected Corporate Secretary of a major Corporation, as told to the author by Honor Moore Muller. This is her story. It is a "Greatest Generation" tale beginning in 1928 when two of her four older brothers delivered her into the world and named her, "Honor."

During the nineteen years I have known her, I have been intrigued, over and over, by the 1,001 stories of her life and rise to the top. She likes to talk and I am a good listener. I kept telling her that she should write the story of her life and times. During my retirement I spent many hours writing 5 books. I decided that if she wouldn't write it, I would. Her story is a delightful compilation of charming events. She is a role model for young ladies, showing that it is possible for them to achieve success no matter how humble their beginnings.

She didn't think her life was so exceptional; I did. I'm certain that when you've read this book, you will agree. Certainly, a lady with such secretarial experience would be well qualified to be a writer on her own. She finally felt inspired; at least, to sit down and draft the input. I had convinced her that her story would be best told by another to avoid her being accused of being an egotist, because, as you read on, you will note that her character is worthy of much praise and admiration. I call her my angel. She has been a blessing during my last quarter of life. All who know her love her for her outgoing, loyal, caring nature.

American women have been struggling for equality for over a century. The husband was the wage earner and the wife was the homemaker. A girl's traditional goal was to find a husband, have children and take care of the family. That all changed with the times. Women began standing up for their rights. They marched for the right to vote. During both World Wars I and II, they replaced the men who had gone off to war. They joined the work force and proved their ability to do many of the jobs outside of the home that only men had been doing.

Slowly, but surely, women were moving into what was a man's world. Women were not only doing a man's work but they were taking over their higher positions.

In 2019 women are officers in charge of giant corporations and captains on commercial aircraft. They are sailors, soldiers, aviators, astronauts, and Marines, not just in uniform, but in combat and space exploration.

Honor is an example of those women of her generation. She rose through the ranks of Southern California Edison to become the Corporate Secretary, the first woman Corporate Officer in the company. How she got there on her own ability is the theme of this story and its rewards.

*Charles Franklin Hutchins*
*Carmel, CA 2019*

# Cast of Characters

## Honor's bosses:

Manager of Accounting and Budgeting - Leonard Muller - 1946
Manager of the Hydro Division - Gil Woodman - 1946-48
Executive Department - V.P and Engineer - Noel Hinson - 1950 (Age 21)
Vice President of Industrial Relations - Raymond G. Kenyon - 1951
President and CEO - Harold Quinton - 1954 - 1957
President and CEO - Jack Horton - 1959 - 1979
Executive Vice President - Finance - H. Frederick Christie - 1979 - 1984
Executive Vice President - Finance - John E. Bryson - 1984 - 1986

## Edison Officers -1984

Management Committee
    Howard P. Allen
    David J. Fogarty
Senior Vice Presidents
    Michael R. Peevey
    L.T. Papay
    P. L. Martin
Vice Presidents
    Robert H. Bridenbecker
    Glenn J. Bjorkllund
    Charles B. McCarthy, Jr.
Vice Presidents
    Joe T. Head, Jr.
    Kenneth P Baskin
    Harold B. Ray
Vice Presidents
    Edward A. Myers, Jr.
    Robert Dietsch
    Robert E. Umbaugh
    C.E. Hathaway
Vice President and Controller - Richard K. Bushey
Vice President and General Counsel - John R. Bury
**Secretary - HONOR (Moore) MULLER**
Vice President and Treasurer - Michael L. Noel
    *—As of 2016, six of the above had passed away.*

## Co-workers

Harold Kelley - Building Manager - Both locations.
George Hanawalt - District Manager
Kathy (Howard) Allen - Executive Secretary to President and CEO-1951
Marie Tyerman - Marketing Department Kitchen Designer
Mary (Poulos) Doufas - Honor's Secretary
Vilma Sinclair - Secretary to the Director of Executive Development
The Officers and Employees of Southern California Edison Company

## The Moore Family

| | |
|---|---|
| Mahlon - Father | 1884-1964 |
| Henrietta - Mother | 1888-1958 |
| Aunt Lilly - Mother's sister | 1886-1980 |
| Uncle Billy - Mother's brother | 1873-1943 |
| Claude - Brother | 1909-1995 |
| Aubrey - Brother | 1912-2000 |
| Lillian - Sister | 1916-2002 |
| Mahlon - Brother | 1919-1997 |
| Milton - Brother | 1924-1987 |
| Margaret - Sister | 1926-2015 |
| Honor | 1928- |

## The Muller Family

| | |
|---|---|
| Otto Muller - Len's brother | 1909-1991 |
| Nita Muller - Otto's wife | 1913-2010 |
| Leonard (Len) - Honors's husband | 1910-1999 |
| Brian - Len's Son | 1940-2010 |
| Marion - Len's Sister | 1914-2009 |
| Lotie Smith - Marion's husband | 1911-1995 |

## Friends and Contacts in England

Ian and Hilare Pulford - Rector of Coberley
Kathleen and Pat Barnett - Executive Assistant - Borax Ltd, London
Olive and Roy Watson - Pen Pal of Len's Wife
Dr. Margaret Pawson - Escort to "All Creatures Great and Small" PBS TV Series Site in the Yorkshire area.

# Contents

*Through The Glass Ceiling    i*
*Dedication    iii*
*Prologue    v*
*Cast of Characters    vii*

## The First Rung
### Character Building

Chapter 1 – Roots    5
Chapter 2 – The Moore Family    7
Chapter 3 – Childhood Memories    9
Chapter 4 – Sisters    13
Chapter 5 – Uncle Billy    17

## The Second Rung
### Education and War

Chapter 6 – Hudson High    21
Chapter 7 – The Home Front    25
Chapter 8 – The Moore Brothers' War    27

## The Third Rung
### Time to Launch a Career

Chapter 9 – California Bound - 1946    37
Chapter 10 – Honor's Job Hunt    39
Chapter 11 – Up The Career Ladder    45
Chapter 12 – Life in the Office    47
Chapter 13 – The Hierarchy    51

# The Fourth Rung
## Self Improvement

Chapter 14 – Harvard Business School   55
Chapter 15 – Social Life   59
Chapter 16 – Len Muller - Biography   63
Chapter 17 – Marriage - 1964   67
Chapter 18 – Life Out of The Office   69
Chapter 19 – Dodgers' Fan   85

# The Fifth Rung
## Success

Chapter 20 – Corporate Secretary - September 20, 1979   91
Chapter 21 – Honor's Decision To Retire   97
November 20, 1986   97
Chapter 22 – Being Retired with Len   103
Chapter 23 – Honor's Letter To Vice-President Bush   105
Chapter 24 – Widowhood - April 16, 1999   115
Chapter 25 – Charles - 2001   117
Chapter 26 – Corresponding With
President George H.W. Bush - 2009   123
Chapter 27 – Remembering Lil and Bob - 2002   127
Chapter 28 – Remembering Margaret   129
Chapter 29 – The Last Moore   131
Chapter 30 – Role Model   133

*Epilogue   135*

# Figures

1a - Hudson River at Hudson, New York     *5*
1b - The Hudson "Athens" Lighthouse at Hudson, New York     *6*
2 - The Moore Family     *7*
3 - Bob and Lil Rufi     *13*
4 - Margaret Lois Moore     *14*
5 - Joan, Honor, Judy, and Jean     *21*
6 - Honor as a teenager     *22*
7 - Sample of WWII Ration Cards     *24*
8 - Claude Moore and his daughter Peggy     *27*
9 - Aubrey Moore - With Susan and Sandra     *28*
10 - Mahlon Moore     *29*
11 - Ensign Milton Moore     *30*
12 - "Milt" Moore and His Crew and Their ***"Avenger"*** Bomber     *31*
13 - Celebrating War's End     *32*
14 - Honor's Year Book Graduation Photo and List of School Activities     *34*
15 - Lions Club Octet - 1944     *34*
16 - Honor at Lil and Bob Kernan's house in Burbank, California - 1946     *39*
17 - Jack Horton     *56*
18 - Len Muller     *63*
19 - Honor and Len - wedding     *67*
20 - "Vin" Scully in the Broadcast Booth at Dodger Stadium, L.A.     *85*
21a - CEO's Letter to the Officers and Department Heads: Honor's Election - 1979     *91*
21b - SCE Press Release     *92*
22 - Southern California Edison Executive Officers as of 1984     *95*
23 - CEO's Nomination of Honor for 1985 YWCA Silver Achievement Award     *96*
24 - Honor's Letter of Resignation - November 20, 1986     *97*
25 - Board of Directors Acknowledgement Resolution - Page 1 of 2     *98*
25 - Letter, Board of Directors' Resolution - Page 2 of 2     *99*
26 - Invitation to Honor's Retirement Party     *100*
27a - Honor's Retirement Party with Family – November 13, 1986     *101*
27b - Honor and Jack Horton     *101*

27c - Honor and Len in Retirement     *103*
28 - Milton (Milt) Moore - V. P. George H.W. Bush with Milt     *105*
29a - Honor's Letter to Vice President Bush     *106*
29b - Honor's Letter to Vice President Bush     *107*
30 - V.P. Bush's Reply – March 27, 1987     *108*
31 - V.P. George and Barbara Bush - Christmas - 1988     *109*
32 - Bellingham House - 1989 –1991     *110*
33 - Honor and Mally and the View from Bellingham House     *110*
34 - Mally's 75th birthday. April 5, 1994, Fair Oaks, California     *111*
35 - Honor at age 68 and Mickey at age 70 in 1996     *112*
35a - Mahlon (Mally) Horatio Moore Jr.- April 5, 1919-December 21, 1997     *113*
36 - Len's Memorial Service Bulletin     *115*
37 - Charles Franklin Hutchins, Lt. Colonel, U.S. Army, Retired     *117*
38 - Honor with Charles     *121*
39 - Honor At Home     *121*
40a - Charles Letter To President George H.W. Bush - March, 2009 - Page 1 of 2     *123*
40b - Charles Letter to President George H,W, Bush-March 2009 - Page 2 of 2     *124*
41 - President Bush's Reply.- May, 2009     *125*
42 - Honor's "Thank You" Letter to President Bush     *126*
43 - Lillian (Lil) Moore Rufi and Robert (Bob) Glenn Rufi     *127*
44 - Honor's Home, since 1991, and Her New, 2014 Mercedes     *128*
45 - Margaret (Mickey) Lois Moore holding "Maisie"     *129*
46 - Mickey's son, Spencer Nilson, delivering Mickey's ashes to the wind and sea     *130*
47 - The Seven Moore siblings At Milt's house In Glendale, CA - 1984     *131*
48 - Charles and Honor **CHEERS!**     *135*

# Through The Glass Ceiling

## Honor Moore Muller
*as told to*
## Charles Franklin Hutchins

# The First Rung
## Character Building

# Chapter 1 – Roots

EVERY SUCCESSFUL PERSON seems to have been born and raised in small town America. Our generation, the "Greatest Generation," comprised the population of the USA during the Twentieth Century. 1928 was a good year to be born. The "War To End All Wars" had ended ten years before then and life was peaceful and predictable.

My name is Charles. I was born in 1927. The lady I'm going to tell you about was born seven months later in 1928. We spent our childhoods during the Great Depression of the 1930's; Honor in Hudson, New York, and I, in Gaylord, Michigan; both small towns, about the same size and located at about the same latitude. At that latitude, there are four distinct seasons; not so in California.

We had a lot in common besides our environment. Our respective spouses died in 1999. We met two years later and have been "dating" ever since. Honor is too humble to tell you her story, I had to convince her. She is not one to live in the past or to talk about herself. We are both Presbyterians. We both sing in the choir. We both love watching movies.

Fig. 1 - a Hudson River at Hudson, New York

The small town of Hudson lies on the east side of the Hudson River 125 miles north of New York City. It was the first chartered city in the United States in 1785 after the signing of the Declaration of Independence. It had been a whaling port in the early 1800's despite its location so far up the Hudson River from the ocean. Its principal industry revolved around two cement plants located just outside the city limits. There were two banks, two movie theaters, plus a few local taverns. Honor's father was the proprietor of one of the two laundries in town. There was also a "Red-Light District," which is part of the city's "scarlet past." Otherwise, it was the type of community and life-style depicted by Norman Rockwell in his magazine art. This was Honor's environment from 1928 to 1946.

The New York Central Railroad runs adjacent to the Hudson River on the east shore. Route 9 ran beside the railroad and was the main artery for highway travel from New York City, through Hudson, north to the Canadian border. Now, the New York State Thruway and the Taconic Parkway provide speedier highway travel through the New York and New England States.

The Rip Van Winkle Bridge spans the river from Hudson to the city of Catskill on the west shore. The Bridge was named after Rip Van Winkle, the legendary character created by author Washington Irving of Tarrytown, New York. Lore has it that hen-pecked Rip Van Winkle slept for twenty years in the Catskill Mountains. The bridge was the gateway to the many ski resorts and summer spas in the Catskill Mountains. It was a mecca for New Yorkers as a "get-away" from New York City. Many entertainers got their start performing in the Catskill resorts.

Fig. 1-b The Hudson "Athens" Lighthouse at Hudson, New York

# Chapter 2 – The Moore Family

Fig. 2 - The Moore Family
Standing, left to right: Mahlon, Claude, Milton, and Aubrey
Seated, left to right: Honor, Margaret, Mother Henrietta, and Lillian

HONOR WAS THE YOUNGEST of seven children, four boys and three girls. As I write this, Honor is the last survivor. As Honor tells it, if the "pill" had been available in those years, she wouldn't have been born, nor would her sister Margaret, (Mickey), or her brother Milton (Milt). After having four children, her mother had not planned to have more children. Mickey was two years older than Honor and they were very close throughout their lives—"sisters and best friends"—as Honor characterizes their relationship.

Honor's mother, Henrietta Dohrmann, was of German descent. Her father, Mahlon Moore, was of Scots/Irish descent. Mahlon started the family business, the New Method Laundry, one of two laundries in Hudson. Several ladies were employed to operate the mangle and to do the ironing as needed. Honor remembers, as a child, that she and Mickey were fascinated watching the mangle in operation. They would watch a team of ladies feed the sheets into the mangle, then run around to the other side to watch the pressed sheets come out and be folded by another team.

All four brothers worked, either part-time or full time at the laundry, delivering or picking up customer laundry. Sister Lillian (Lil) worked part-time in the office.

The Moores had two laundry delivery trucks and a family car. Honor's brother, Mahlon (Jr.) (Mally) would round up the the neighborhood kids and drive them out to the local swimming hole called "Buttermilk Falls." She tells of a man, diving off the side of a rocky cliff who misjudged his water target and hit his head on a jutting rock. He survived, but he bled profusely. *Mally called our group to get out of the pool and back in the truck so that we could get him to the local hospital for treatment; it required a few stitches in his head. It was a memorable experience for the younger kids, as they had to swim through bloody water to exit the pool.*

Honor learned to swim the hard way. She was challenged to swim out to the raft. She was a brave, confident swimming novice. She just made it, without any help. I'll let her tell about it:

*A big part of our summer fun was the family outing to Lake Taconic, a State Park. There was a raft, or float, on the lake, and as a 'rite of passage,' we all had the goal of swimming out to the float, into the deep water. Being the youngest of the family, I was the last to accomplish this feat. On the day I felt up to the swim, Mickey and Milt escorted me. As we neared the float, some teenage boys were having a good time splashing and ducking each other. I gulpd some water as a result of their antics, but Milt said, 'You're OK, just keep stroking, we're almost there.' And so I did. and was glad to be able to hoist myself up on the raft. When I had reached the steps, Milt said, 'You made it!'*

*The lifeguard on the shore had observed their antics and rowed his boat out to ask if I was OK. Milt assured him that I was. Then he asked if I wanted a ride to shore with him. Milt, Mickey and I, in unison, said, 'No thank you.' After I had reached the float, I stood up and waved at Mom and Aunt Lilly sitting at our picnic table. They waved their approval. After Milt and Mickey had taken a few dives from the diving board, we swam back to shore. The lap was a 'breeze' as I was pretty full of confidence, I gave myself a mental badge."*

# Chapter 3 – Childhood Memories

IN 1991, HONOR WROTE THIS opening introduction to a collection of memorabilia that she had written, in one of her Travelers Journals, to Mickey on her 65th birthday, about their lives and travels together

### The Way We Were
(A collection of "growing up" remembrances
for Mickey on this special day, April 16, 1991)

---

*The Way We Were*
*Remembering the joy of*
*sharing a large portion of our*
*life's journey, and wishing you*
*all the joy for the*
*"travels" ahead*
*Much, much Love, Honor*

---

*The most vivid memory of growing*
*up together had to do with anything shared.*
*Mickey always gave her little sister the larger portion.*

---

*Time for Honor to start school*
*After all the anticipation of finally*
*getting to go to school like the*
*other family members. Kindergarten*
*overwhelmed me! You and Milt (Brother)*
*took turns "Dropping me off" at*
*Kindergarten because I fussed and*
*cried and didn't want to be left*
*without you or Milt.*

*Playing next door to the Websters you fell
from the utility pole, dropping yourself
on the iron pipe that bordered the lawn
Seeing you so "lifeless, I ran home and
cryng, announced to "Mom" that you just
killed youself when you fell!*

*Another fall you took, during play,
and Aunt Lilly, trying to soothe
the hurt, said, "It's all right, you
just lost your balance." When the crying
continued, Milt, trying to reassure you, said
"Don't cry Honey, you just lost your
balance, and I will help you find it
tomorrow."*

*We loved to watch our big sister, Lil,
(our oldest sister) getting dressed for a date
Watching from upstairs that night, Lil
hosted a pre-dance gathering at
14 Glenwood, (Moore home) we were fascinated
to watch the guests arrive and see
the girls in their beautiful evening gowns
We both agreed that our sister was the
most beautiful of all.*

*Lil provided our Allowance money
in exchange for simple chores
Mine being to brush Lil's suede shoes with
a little wire brush. You were
delegated more delicate duties
such as, washing Lil's silk hosiery, etc.*

*Talking and giggling in bed while
Mom and the 'Adult' children played
cards downstairs, periodically, we would
hear, 'Girls, stop talking and and go to sleep'.
Then, a test—'girls, we are going to get
some ice cream, what kind would you like?'
You (Mickey) were too smart to jump at the bait,
but I quickly shouted, 'Chocolate!'
And then, from downstairs, 'That's what I
thought ... Now **go to sleep!**'*

# Chapter 4 – Sisters

*"A sister is part of your heart and most of your memories."*

Fig. 3 - Bob and Lil Rufi

**Lillian (Lil) Anita Moore** was the first of three daughters of the seven children in the Moore family. All the children grew up in Hudson, but left during or after WWII. She married Robert (Bob) Kernan after the war, in 1945. Robert was her boss at Lockheed where they met during the war. They had a baby girl named Linda Honor Kernan who was born prematurely. Sadly, she died within 48 hours. Bob Kernan died December 24, 1962, at age 49. Lil remained a widow for 9 years.

Lil married Robert (Bob) Rufi on February 26, 1971. (Brother Milt's birthday). Bob was a pilot Veteran of WWII. His unit was due to embark for Europe just as the war ended. He joked that "The enemy heard I was coming!" Bob held the land speed record for 1946 at the Bonneville Salt Flats in a car that he built himself. He cast the manifold and found some wheels from an old WWI "Jenny" aircraft.

He and Lil built a cement hull sailboat and lived on it for 4 years. Lil had a stroke. They sold the boat and a small condo and bought a house in Pismo Beach with a view of the Pacific Ocean.

Lil died April 14, 2002, at Arroyo Grande Care Center, two days before her 86th birthday. Bob died one month later on May 13, 2002.

**Margaret (Mickey) Lois Moore** was the sixth child of Henrietta and Mahlon Moore. She was two years older than Honor. Margaret was two years ahead of Honor in school. When she graduated from high school in 1944, she immediately went to work as secretary to the president and CEO of a local company, V&O Press Co, a company allied with national companies providing services to the WWII war effort. The woman she succeeded as secretary left abruptly to join her husband who was in the U.S. Army serving in another state.

It was imperative that she fill this vacancy immediately. She had to report to work the day after graduation, but because the Senior Ball was that night, she was allowed to take the the next morning off and report for work at 1:00 p.m. Margaret was an outstanding student and was recommended without hesitation by the Student Advisor when called by the V&O Press Company to fill the vacancy. She remained with V&O for 2 years. She had mastered secretarial skills and in this job position, she learned administrative skills which were invaluable to her for the rest of her life in subsequent jobs, including being involved in the "start-up" of her husband's business.

After moving to Los Angeles, Margaret had varied work experiences as secretary to lawyers and owners of construction companies. She was quickly employed as Executive Secretary and Administrator to Ted Hermann of Hermann Company, a construction company known for its participation in additions to the Rose Bowl, among other major projects. When the Company relocated, she took a position at Kerr Glass Company.

Fig. 4 - Margaret Lois Moore

In 1953, she married Spencer Nilson and became a "stay at home mom" following the birth of their daughter, Lisa Ellen, in June 1954. Their son, Spencer Evan, was born in February 1957.

Her "skill set" was put back to work when Spencer started his own successful company, "The Nilson Report." He was founder, owner and president. The company published information relating to credit-card ownership and marketing. They divorced in 1976, maintaining an amicable, non-hostile, relationship, while enjoying their children, and later, their grandchildren. Margaret died on May 26, 2015 in Santa Barbara, California, where she had lived for twenty years following her retirement.

# Chapter 5 – Uncle Billy

HONOR'S MOTHER HAD A brother known to the Moore family as "Uncle Billy." He was a bachelor and lived with the family. He and Honor's mother had a small inheritance from their father's estate receiving payments twice a year from the Trust. He worked part-time in the family laundry; otherwise, he enjoyed hobnobbing with his cronies in the local taverns. He also helped with the younger children. He would often pick up Honor after school. The route home was not direct; a stop at his favorite tavern was not unusual. Honor enjoyed the pretzels while Uncle Billy enjoyed his beer and conversation with his friends. Honor shared this memory of time spent with him in her own words:

*Uncle Billy was my mother's oldest brother. He was born on May 29, 1873 in New York City. His given name was John Henry Dorhmann, but for some reason, he was "Uncle Billy" to us. He was the eldest of seven children and my mother was the youngest. He never married, remained a bachelor all his life and lived in our home. He was loved by all of us in our family and endeared himself to all the children in our neighborhood who also considered him their "Uncle Billy." My sister, Margaret (Mickey) and I, asked him about his given name and why we called him "Uncle Billy?" He responded by saying, "Yes, I am called by several names, and that is fine with me, as long as you don't call me late for dinner."*

*One of my earliest memories of Uncle Billy was when he used to pick me up at school to walk me home. Sometimes, in winter, he would bring my sled along to pull me home. Our route home was rarely direct. Sometimes we would detour to one of his favorite local taverns. He would sit me up at the bar and buy me a ginger ale, which came with an unlimited supply of pretzels. He would enjoy a beer (or two) and converse with his cronies. When we arrived home, later than expected by Mom, she would ask,"What took you so long?" knowing full well, what took us so long. I would then, proudly, pull my supply of pretzels out of my pocket and show them to her. She would say, "That's just what I thought!"*

*Uncle Billy was familiar with all the local taverns, and, of course, I was, as well. Many years later, after I was married, when my oldest brother, Claude,* met my husband, he said to him, "Len, did Honor ever tell you that she had been in every bar in Hudson by the time she was five years old?" That is when Len learned about the legendary Uncle Billy.

Another clear memory of Uncle Billy relates to my Junior High School years (Grades 7 and 8).

One day, while sitting in class, I was nudged by a classmate who pointed to the door. The upper glass portion revealed Uncle Billy, gently knocking on the door. The teacher let him in and, upon politely removing his hat, identified himself saying, "I came to deliver Honor Moore's lunch." With some embarrassment, I left my seat and thanked him, taking my lunch back to my seat. Of course, all eyes were focused on this episode. Our teacher also thanked him for coming. With that, he doffed his hat saying, 'Goodbye, Teacher," turned to the class and said, "Goodbye, Class" and departed. Laughter and smiles a-plenty from the class enjoying the interruption, and then, it was back to work.

On another occasion, following the Friday morning "Assembly Program," attended by all the students, we were exiting the Auditorium, there was Uncle Billy. sitting in the back row, enjoying the program along with the students. The reason for his presence this time, was to deliver my forgotten locker key. My fellow students found Uncle Billy charming and his visits a delight. When he died, many of them came to the Funeral Home to sign the Guest Book and express their condolences. He was everybody's Uncle Billy.

# The Second Rung
## Education and War

# Chapter 6 – Hudson High

Fig. 5 - Joan, Honor, Judy, and Jean

Honor And Her Classmates - 8th Grade – 1942

STUDENTS IN THE EARLY Forties had a choice of three types of curricula: Academic (College Prep), Commercial or Industrial Arts. Such options were quite common throughout the nation. They were in my high school as well. Since college was not an option for Honor, she selected the Commercial Course. Several of her classmates did go on to college following graduation. During the war many of the male graduates enlisted in a branch of the armed services. The young women found employment locally at the telephone company as telephone switchboard operators, secretaries and office workers. Honor's scholastic grades qualified her for college entrance, but it was not affordable for her family.

As it turned out, the skills she developed taking the Commercial course prepared her well for the future that was destined to be a rewarding career. The classes included typing, shorthand, office etiquette and business arithmetic. She would have liked to have taken a foreign language, but that was limited to students enrolled in the Academic courses.

The War years were "Big Band" years. Honor loved to dance and enjoyed the opportunities during those years. She still dances. She was, and is, a big Glenn Miller fan and enjoys listening to Glenn Miller music. Schools went all out to provide opportunities to experience the "social graces" like dances following basketball games, as well as Sophomore, Junior and Senior class Proms. There were Clubs, sports, dramatics and other non-academic activities to add to required classwork. She had wanted to learn how to play the piano. However, professional instruction was not available to her. Her brother Aubrey paid for lessons for her sister Mickey until he got married and left home. Mickey did help her by passing on what she had learned to Honor. She did take piano lessons after she retired.

West Point Military Academy is about 70 miles south of Hudson. Honor recalls attending football games there as a member of her Girl Scout Troop. It seemed to her that the Troop Leaders were more interested in the Cadets than they were in the games. Scout training, as a teenager, is another character builder to be noted in her upbringing.

Fig. 6 - Honor as a teenager

The Troop had a Camp on a nearby lake called Camp Van Buren. Across the lake was a Jewish boy's camp; conveniently equipped with row-boats available to the boy's young councilors. President Van Buren's home is located in Kinderhook, in close proximity to the lake.

Van Buren was the 8th U.S. President, from 1837 to 1841. The lake was within driving distance. It was, also, where the kids went swimming in the summer time.

She showed her outgoing nature by joining the school Cheer-Leading Squad. She was well suited mentally and physically to engage in any sport. She had a talent for singing. The school had an "A Capella" choir. Both Honor and Mickey were members. They also sang in their Presbyterian Church choir.

Honor had several part-time jobs while in high school; this was one of them:

*On my first day working for a local business man, owner of an insurance agency, I was given the task of stamping calendars with Mr. Thorn's agency's name and address and placing them in envelopes for mailing to his clients. I was taking this task quite seriously when I realized my brothers Milt and Mally were standing outside my window mimicking me stamping the calendars! Nothing like brothers to help you not to take yourself too seriously.!*

*The part-time jobs I had were when I was in High School taking a "Business" course. Since my grades warranted it, I had the opportunity to work two afternoons a week in the office of a local business man. The good news was that I was paid for the job, but the down-side was that I missed out on being included in certain photos for our year book, including extra-curricular activities such as the Cheerleading Team, A Capella Choir and Thespians.*

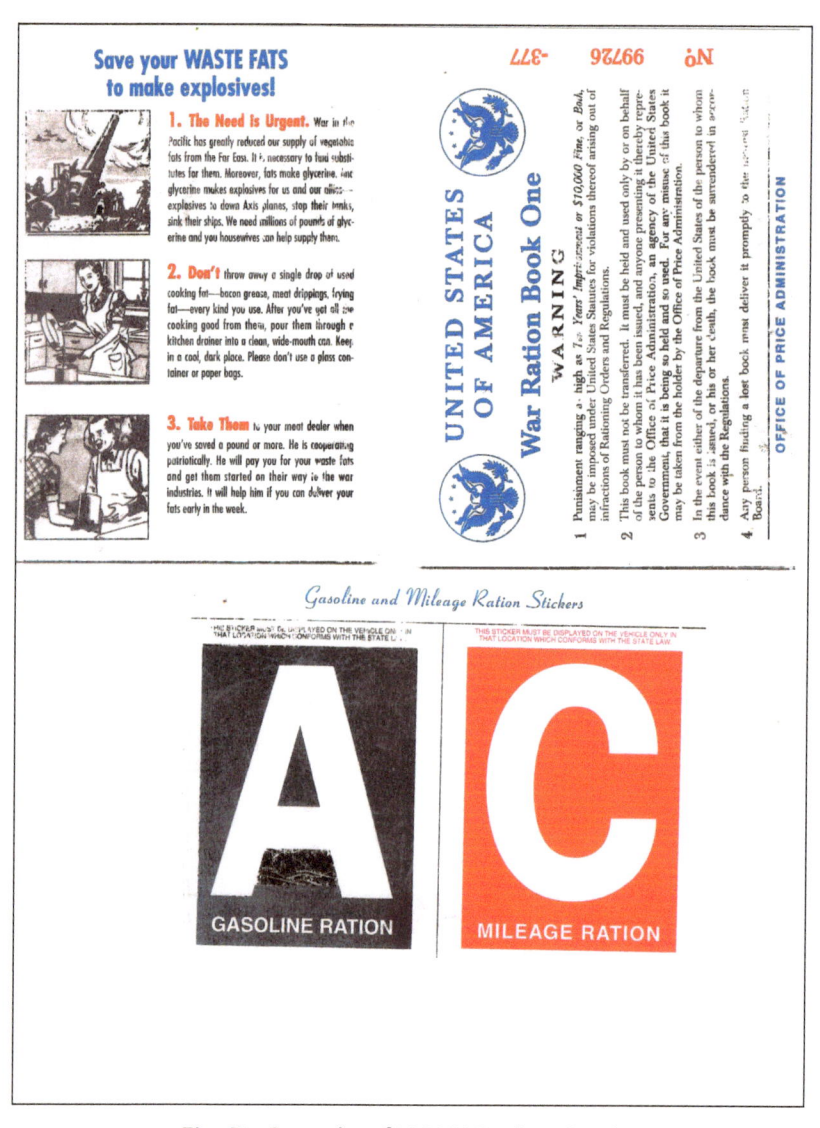

Fig. 7 - Sample of WWII Ration Cards

# Chapter 7 – The Home Front

*What was it like for the Moore family during "The Great Depression?*

RAILROADS RAN THROUGH small towns. Good men, looking for work, took advantage of the free transportation provided by empty boxcars to get around. We were innocent kids back then. My next younger brother and I, used to hop a freight car for the adventure of "Riding The Rails." We would catch the morning train and ride from Gaylord, 27 miles to Grayling, Michigan. Then back home on the evening run. Just a couple of 8 and 10 year old kids mixed in with men. They would treat us with kindness, and concern for our safety. That's the kind of men that were of that generation. These same jobless men would have to ask for food from homes at stops along the route. Back then, people seldom locked their doors. Hobo camps were common near freight yards.

Honor remembers an occasional "Hobo" appearing at their back kitchen door, asking for somethng to eat. Her mother would let him come in through the screen door, into the kitchen, and sit down at the table for whatever she happened to have available. She might even send him off with a bite to eat. It was caring like this that was common in those days. The Moore children were brought up in an environment of moral values, when families stuck together and most people lived according to the law and the Golden Rule. We were one people, innocent, trusting, simple, honest and patriotic. That's when America was "Great." That was Honor's background as a teenager. It has stood her in good stead throughout her life.

Then came the War. There was work for all, including "Rosie The Riveter." the Depression was ended. WWII was won by people who carried those principles through to "Victory" and recovery. The men were impelled to serve their country. To "Dodge the Draft" branded you as a coward to be despised. The women kept the home fires burning and the letters coming. To be classified as physically,"4-F" was a disappointment to those so anxious to serve. They found other ways to serve, or, their skills were essential to the War effort. Students were deferred to complete their education. Honor remembers that several young men in her high school left to "sign up" for military duty. After the war, they returned to get their diplomas with her class in 1946. Honor's brothers were old enough to join immediately.

The war in the Pacific greatly reduced our supply of rubber. Tires were now synthetic rubber. Items in short supply were needed at the "Front." Almost everything had to be rationed. Boy Scouts collected scrap metal. Waste cooking fat was saved in the kitchen to make glycerin to make explosives. High School boys enlisted as soon as they graduated. Men from the age of 18 to to 35 were eligible for the draft and had to Register. Honor's 4 brothers volunteered and served throughout the War.

In the meantime, we kids were just starting high school. I joined the Boy Scouts and The Sea Scouts. Physical training in school was mandatory. We boys learned to march and play soldier. We couldn't wait to join up. Many quit school early, lied about their age, and enlisted. As soon as I graduated in January 1946, I enlisted for two years in the Regular Navy. Just in time to qualify as a WWII Veteran, "Ruptured Duck" and all.

# Chapter 8 – The Moore Brothers' War

WWII STARTED DECEMBER 7, 1941 with the sneak attack at Pearl Harbor, Territory of Hawaii. It ended with the Atom bomb attacks on Hiroshima and Nagasaki, Japan in 1945. In the meantime, Honor was attending Hudson High School. She had 4 older brothers; Aubrey, Claude, Mahlon and Milton. Everybody wanted to be a part of the war effort. The Moore boys were all draft age and like their contemporaries, they didn't hesitate; they volunteered. They survived the war.

Fig. 8 - Claude Moore and his daughter Peggy

**SGT Claude Richard Moore** served in the U.S. Army during WWII in a limited capacity due to a hearing impairment. He enlisted, despite a medical classification of 4F that would have exempted him from the Draft. He was stationed at Fort Benning, Georgia for the duration.

> *Claude was the eldest brother of our family of seven children. When his three younger brothers signed up to serve in World War II (WWII), he wanted to be in uniform, as well. He had a hearing deficit as a result of scarlet fever as a child. He was not drafted, but signed up to serve, as his brothers had. Due to his hearing impairment, he was assigned to duties at Fort Benning, Georgia where he remained for the duration of the war. The high point for him, while serving in a non-combat role, was that he had the opportunity of participating*

*in his brothers' achievements. Our brother, Mahlon (Infantry), was accepted for Officer Candidate School (OCS) at Fort Benning and earned his Commission as an Army 2nd Lieutenant. Claude pinned his bars on him.*

*Later, our brother Aubrey took Paratrooper training there. Claude pinned his Paratrooper wings on him. Milton (Navy pilot), received his commission as Ensign at Chapel Hill, North Carolina. Claude stood up all the way on an over-night train ride to Chapel Hill to pin Milt's wings on him. These events made his stint at Fort Benning worthwhile. He was very proud of his brothers and their combat service.*

Fig. 9 - Aubrey Moore - With Susan and Sandra

**MSGT Aubrey Mahlon Moore** had married in 1940, but, he too, enlisted in the Army and served as a paratrooper in the 82$^{nd}$ Airborne Division. By the end of the war he had been promoted to Master Sergeant. He had two daughters and was the first of the Moore clan to settle in California.

Fig. 10 - Mahlon Moore

**Major Mahlon (Mally) Horatio Moore Jr.** joined the Army and served in the Infantry from 1940 to 1945. He was commissioned out of Officer Candidate School at Fort Benning, Georgia as a 2$^{nd}$ Lieutenant. As a Captain, he went ashore on D-Day in the first wave in France. At the end of the war, he remained in the Army Reserve. He was called back to Active Duty from 1950 to 1952 during the Korean Conflict. He retired from the Army with the rank of Major.

Fig. 11 - Ensign Milton Moore

**Lieutenant (JG) Milton George Moore** was the youngest of the four Moore brothers. He joined the Navy to fly. He was commissioned as a Naval Officer in 1942. He flew the Gruman "*Avenger* TBM" (Torpedo Bomber), the largest single engine plane in the Navy, off the *San Jacinto* CVL 30 Aircraft Carrier. He was assigned to Squadron VT-5, alongside George H.W. Bush. In fact he was flying wing man to George when George was shot down over the Japanese Island of Chichi Jima. They were close friends.

On September 2, 1944, Ensign Milton Moore (Milt) along with Commander Donald Melvin, their Squadron Commander, and Ensign Doug West, attacked the Japanese main communications center on the Island of Chichi Jima, south of the Japanese mainland. Their mission was to drop their bombs on the radio buildings. The island was heavily defended by anti-aircraft weapons. The U.S. Navy had suffered heavy losses trying to knock out the station.

Fig. 12 - "Milt" Moore and His Crew and Their *"Avenger"* Bomber

George Bush "HIS WORLD WAR II YEARS" Photo - Courtesy of Mrs. Jeanne Moore (Milt's wife)

The Gruman *Avenger* was crewed by 3 men. Milt's regular crewmen were Charles Bynum, the turret gunner (shown on the right) and Richard Gorman, his radioman. (on the left). When the four bombers made their pass dropping their bombs, George Bush's ship was hit and went down trailing smoke. Milt was flying on his wing. Bush managed to bail out after ordering his crew to go. Assuming that they had done so, he bailed out. Apparently they hadn't jumped, although it was reported by another plane that they had seen one chute. After the war, Japanese records indicated that two chutes had been seen. They might have been captured. On this mission, the two crewmen on Bush's plane, William G. (Ted) White (Gunner) and John Delany (Radioman) were never seen again.

Overhead, Milt created a diversion when he saw the tell-tale wakes of Japanese patrol boats heading for George in the water. They were heading toward Bush. It was a race against time. Charles Bynum, who was Moore's turret gunner, had a clear view of the action. He said he saw 2 chutes "Our two planes went down and strafed the boats and drove them off. As we (Moore and Melvin) dove I fired my turret gun at them." Milt, then, with his ammunition expended, flew circles in another part of the bay to mislead them until, low on fuel, he had to return the *San Jacinto*.

The submarine, *Finback*, maintaining a rescue station 7 miles off the coast, was stationed there because so many pilots were being shot down during their bombing runs. It arrived on the scene 3 hours later from the other side of the island.

Bush credited Ensign Doug West, also circling, with directing the sub to Bush by aiming his wing at him as he was paddling in his raft towards the surfaced sub. When the sub reached him through a mine field, he was hauled aboard and remained with the sub until it reached its home port. Milt was promoted to Lieutenant (JG).

Fig. 13 - Celebrating War's End
Photo - George Bush "HIS WORLD WAR II YEARS"

At the Oceana Naval Air Station, Virginia: Jacqueline West, Lt (j.g.) George

H.W. Bush, standng, and (Seated left to right) Barbara Bush, DougWest, Bea Guy, Lt. (j.g.) Jack Guy, an unidentified Wave and Lt. (j.g.) Milton Moore; all from Squadron VT-51.

At the end of the war, Milt was Groomsman at George and Barbara's wedding at The First Presbyterian Church in Rye, New York The Bushes visited the Moore's home a few years later..

*George and Barbara, along with their two year old son, George W., paid a visit to Milt and his wife, Emy Lou. During their stay they came to our home to meet Mom, Mickey and me. While we were enjoying coffee and Mom's "famous" cheesecake, Barbara put little George down for a nap in the bedroom that Mickey and I shared. Before his nap was over, he came out of the bedroom and whispered in his mother's ear. She put him on her lap and said something to the effect, "I know that it's a strange bedroom and it's hard for you to go to sleep, but, you must have a nap or you will be too tired to go with us tonight. I will take you back to bed, and remember, you must be very brave." George must have taken her seriously because he did finish his nap.*

*Years later, as the Bush family became so prominent on the political scene, Mickey and I both claimed that "President George W. Bush slept in my bed." (We were not really clear which bed he slept in, Mickey's bed or mine.) It was a delight to meet them. – very warm and easy to know.*

George H.W. Bush and Milt remained lifelong friends.

This is an extract from a *Washington Post* article published the day after George H.W. Bush died :

"What came across was when I went by his grandfather's or uncle's apartment in Manhattan,' recalls Guy. 'It was about the grandest thing I'd ever seen.' Pilot Milton Moore, Bush's best friend in those days, was invited to Greenwich for George's wedding in '45. 'I was very impressed,' says Moore, whose father owned a laundry. Everybody was friendly, but Moore noticed that the young people at the wedding seemed more self-assured than those he knew. No one in Moore's family had even gone to college, but everyone there seemed to talk about college constantly. When introduced, people's colleges were added like extra last names. But Moore always felt comfortable with George. He visited Bush after the war at Yale, and he visited him later in Texas." *Washinton Post–December 2, 2018*

Fig. 14 - Honor's Year Book Graduation Photo and List of School Activities

The local "Lion's' Club" assembled an Octet of Senior High School girls for a benefit program. Honor was one of the girls selected. They brought in a Broadway professional to direct the show. The girls sang three numbers. One of the other acts was a Minstrel Show. Honor is the girl, third from the left, wearing a black skirted gown.

Fig. 15 - Lions Club Octet - 1944

# The Third Rung

## Time to Launch a Career

## Chapter 9 – California Bound - 1946

BACK TO OUR STORY. Up until now, Honor and I have been telling you about the history of her life that constituted the foundation of the life she was about to lead. That's why every element of her life that we have revealed so far has influence on the future course of her career.

She has a remarkable talent for remembering names, dates and circumstances, all of which, any secretary worth her hire, must have at her boss's beck and call to facilitate Company affairs.

The war was over and it was now time for Honor, Mickey and their mom to prepare for their move to Los Angeles. Horace Greeley's famous advice "Go West young man" also applies to young women like Honor. There were limited opportunities for employment in the Hudson area.

Hudson's industry, 2 cement plants, were facing closure due to diminishing limestone reserves and later, environmental issues. The Universal Match Company pulled up stakes and moved to Birmingham, Alabama, taking their jobs with them. After a stagnant and lackluster period, Hudson experienced an unexpected resurgence with an influx of entrepreneurs from New York City. Many purchased second homes in the Hudson area and saw an opportunity for merchandising in the many vacant stores on the main street. Antique dealers, upscale designers and decorators soon occupied the once empty stores generating the interest of tourists.

By 1946, brothers Aubrey, Mally, Milt, and sister Lil were already settled in the greater Los Angeles area of Southern California. Claude had settled in New Jersey before the war. Honor's eldest sister, Lillian, had married Robert (Bob) Kernan in 1945 and was living in California. Honor's mother put their house on the market.

Lil and her husband, Bob Kernan, drove cross-country to Hudson from L.A. to help get the homestead ready for sale. Honor and Mickey made the drive west with Lil and Bob enjoying plenty of sight-seeing along the way. Neither Honor nor Mickey had yet learned to drive, thus could not help with the driving.

Their mother sold their home fairly promptly as there were no new homes built during the war years and returning veterans were in the market to purchase homes and move on with their lives. Their mother stayed behind, temporarily, with Claude and his family in New Jersey for a visit. Claude was the only member of the family who did not move west. Their parents had been separated many years. Their father remained in Hudson where he died in 1964.

At first, Honor and Mickey lived with Lil and Bob in their home in Burbank, a suburb of Los Angeles, until they found jobs. Then they moved to a home in west Hollywood where they rented a room from Bob Kernan's friends. They were fortunate to locate housing close to public transportation and easy access to downtown Los Angeles where they both worked.

In March of 1947 their mother traveled to California by train with her sister (Aunt Lilly), who was part of the family for the next 2 years. In 1948, Henrietta, Mickey and Honor bought a house in Burbank. A year later, Lilly reluctantly left California after receiving an "SOS" call from her sister on the east coast who needed assistance in caring for her husband who was ill with a stroke.

Mickey moved out when she married in July, 1953. They sold the house in 1957 and lived in an apartment until Honor left to attend Radcliffe College in September of that year.

# Chapter 10 – Honor's Job Hunt

Fig. 16 - Honor at Lil and Bob Kernan's house in Burbank, California -1946

What was your goal? To be successful we need to set goals. Honor's response:

*To find a job. I hoped that I would be successful in a job that paid well and offered a future with opportunity and security. Primarily, at this stage of my career, I just wanted a job and I had training and secretarial experience to offer. My mind was focused on doing my best, knowing my future depended upon it, whatever was to come.*

*My decision to apply for a job with the Edison Company was the best decision that I could have made. Those goals were all there just waiting for me to reach and surmount, up one ladder rung at a time. It never occurred to me that I would be employed by the Edison Company for 40 years, much less achieve such a position as an officer, a Corporate Secretary. I never, consciously, set a goal, but that didn't sway my determination to strive to advance to the next rung.*

*My 40-year career with Edison started with a suggestion from my sister Lil. She had noticed an ad in the Los Angeles Times, placed by the Edison Company, for a stenographer. She commented that the Edison building was the building where my sister Mickey would be working if she was hired by a company located in the same building. Mickey's interview for the job was coming up the following week. Lil noted that this was a great location in downtown L.A., right across from the Public Library with the Biltmore Hotel on the opposite corner.*

*Lil's father-in-law, William (B-Bill) Kernan, added that the Edison building was the safest building in town in the event of an earthquake, as it was built with a 3-foot sway. (Every one who comes to California is concerned about the State's earthquake history.) B-Bill had worked for the architectural firm that had designed the building. He had a special connection with this building.*

*The next day, Monday, I went to Edison to apply for the job, remembering the advice from sister Lil and my brothers, Mally and Milt, saying that I should not accept a job as a typist, or file clerk, if offered; but to hold out for a steno position. I had earned top certificates in shorthand and typing and I was up to the task, remembering that old adage that skills need to be exercised or they will be lost; "Use it or lose it."*

*I filled out the employment application and then I was interviewed by the Personnel Manager. He noted that I had only part-time experience and offered me a job as typist. Full of confidence at age 18, I told him I was applying for the job of Stenographer, as advertised in the L.A. Times. I showed him the copy of the ad. He then made a telephone call to the person who had a requisition in for a Stenographer; but, he was away on vacation. He noted that there was another request that might already have been filled. He made a call to Mr. Leonard (Len) Muller, who advised that the position had not been filled, suggesting that he direct the applicant to his office.*

*I was properly attired, wearing a hat and gloves, according to my "Office Etiquette" training.*

*Mr. Muller reviewed my application, noting that I had not yet had a permanent job. He commented that, "In order to get that, you have to start somewhere, don't you?" I agreed. He thought the Operating Department would be a good place to start. He briefly described its function as "The Heartbeat of the Company," since it was responsible for the generation of electricity, Thus, I was offered the job as a stenographer in the "Steno Pool," consisting of one other woman and our woman Supervisor.*

*When he asked when I could start, I suggested, the following Monday, but, he said I would be needed sooner than that! I explained that I lived with my sister and brother-in-law in their home in Burbank and would need to look into the availability of public transportation. He acknowledged that and gave me just one day "to get my act together." After I left Len's office, others commented to Len, "She looks like she just got out of high school." Len said, " She did. This will be her first full time job." I didn't mention the other aspect; I needed to shop for clothes appropriate for the office, to replace my high school togs. The next day my two sisters, Lil and Mickey and I set off for Bullock's Department Store in downtown Los Angeles and managed to select a couple suitable outfits for my new "office wardrobe."*

*Sister Lil had mentioned to me that I would probably find that most people I would meet would be "transplants" from other parts of the country. She pointed out that many, just like our own family, were in California during the war years and decided that California would be their new home. However, that was not the case. Most of my co-workers were native Californians, including my boss, Len Muller. My first day on the job I had a desk in the Steno Pool. The "Ditto" machine also occupied space in this room, thus, there was a considerable amount of traffic coming and going through our office during the day. Mary, our supervisor, introduced me to everyone who came in the room. Everyone that I met was very warm and welcoming, so, I felt my first day was a success.*

When Honor and Mickey first arrived in Burbank, they depended on public transportation to get around for the first year. They found housing that was close to the Pacific Electric System. It was a city-wide, single car, rail system, spread throughout the city and the suburbs. It was divided into divisions identified by colors. Their apartment was close to the "Red" Line. When I was discharged from the Navy at the end of 1947, my buddies and I took the P.E. Trolly from San Pedro into L.A. and on out to Hollywood to see the sights. A few years later, the system was overtaken by the growing post-war volume of buses and cars.

Honor and Mickey used public transportation for the first 5 years to get to work until Mickey was provided a 1949 Ford company car by her boss in 1951; that made the commute more pleasant. When Mickey's employer relocated to Northern California, she remained in Southern California. Honor would ride with Mickey. When Mickey married Spencer Nilson in 1953, Honor bought the car; her first automobile. Her next car was a 1956 Ford Victoria.

*My first duties included typing up reports and forms. When Mr. Muller needed a steno, he would call Mary, supervisor of the Steno Pool, on the interoffice telephone and ask her to send one of us in. After about a week on the job, he suggested that it was about time to start the next phase of the job; taking dictation. I remember, when he finished his first batch of dictation, he suggested that I type it in "draft form." That was a good way to start for both of us. When he gave me the work back, he told me it was ready for final form. He added, "Oh, by the way, everything needs to be dated," he said with a smile. I was somewhat embarrassed that I had overlooked the obvious. From then on, I was assigned most of the dictation duties. Madeleine, my fellow steno, somewhat relieved, said her shorthand skill was a little "rusty." In addition to our work for Mr. Muller, we were assigned to typing reports and memos for others in the department.*

*After almost two years in the Steno Pool, I had the opportunity to be assigned to the Hydro Division of the Operating Department. There were seven men in the group and I was their "Girl Friday" steno performing secreterial duties. I took dictation, principally, from Mr. Gil Woodman, the Division Superintendent. This was a special group of men and we established a great rapport working together. I had my 21st birthday while I was in Hydro. I was treated "royally," with a bouquet of flowers on my desk, a beautiful corsage and a special lunch treat at the Biltmore Hotel. Some in the Operating Department referred to our Hydro group as, "Honor and her Seven Dwarfs."*

*After another 2 years time I had my next opportunity for advancement. I was selected to be secretary to Mr. Noel Hinson, Vice-President and Executive Engineer. This was a fairly short assignment, as Mr. Hinson retired at the end of that year, 1950. I regretted that I had only 10 months to have this opportunity to work for him. He was a very bright man with a wonderful sense of humor.*

*He had many unique stories to tell after his long career at Edison. I learned so much from him. Fortunately, I did not lose that connection. He and his wife, Lois, remained close friends. We enjoyed getting together occasionally on a social basis. Lois and I remained friends even after Mr. Hinson's death, until her death many years later.*

*I remained in the Executive Department, following Mr. Hinson's retirement, to fill in as a substitute secretary as needed. This period of being "unassigned" was somewhat discouraging to me.*

*I even had thoughts of leaving Edison and seeking employment elsewhere. Fortunately, my mother and my sister Mickey prevailed in their counsel regarding my current status. They pointed out that having invested 5 years with Edison, I should give this situation at least 6 months. A wise choice, because the following month, a vacancy opened for a secretary to Mr. Raymond G. Kenyon, Vice-President of Labor and Industrial Relations. I applied for the job and was selected.*

*During the time I was his secretary the Company's 2 labor unions, the IBEW, representing the electrical workers and the CIO, representing the steam station employees, called a "Strike" against the Company. The Strike lasted over 2 months before a settlement was reached between the unions and management. As a salaried employee, I stayed at work with Mr. Kenyon. It was an adventure to be somewhat involved in the dispute; a first labor strike for Edison Company.*

# Chapter 11 – Up The Career Ladder

In 1954 she was faced with a decision that would prove to be a major step up the ladder. She was working for Mr. Kenyon. As you remember, he was Vice President in charge of Personnel and Labor Relations. She liked her position and she liked working for him. However, she was made an offer that tested her loyalty.

*I had an opportunity to climb up another rung of the ladder. Mr. Harold Quinton, President and CEO, met with Mr. Kenyon to let him know he would like to offer me the job of second secretary in his office. He had been elected President of our Industry Association, which entailed more demands on his time and that of his long-time secretary. When Mr. Kenyon told me about this, I told him that I felt privileged to be asked, but I wasn't sure that I wanted to leave him and my current job. He too, had been a wonderful boss with whom I had a great relationship. He looked at me and said, "Sister Moore, take it from Kenyon, you never say 'No' to the President!" He went on to remind me of what a great growth opportunity this would be for a young woman my age (26). He then added, "You have a valuable asset; you take your job seriously, but, not yourself. I credit your mother for that, and growing up in a large family."*

*Thus, the dye was cast for my next career experience.*

The Southern California Edison Company building was located in downtown Los Angeles at the corner of 5th and Grand Avenue. The Los Angeles Public Library and the Biltmore Hotel were located across the street. The building was built in the early 1930"s. At the time it was the tallest building in Los Angeles.

The Lobby décor was impressive with its extensive display of mahogany and marble. The six elevators had mahogany interiors reflecting beautiful craftsmanship not seen in today's architecture. There were thirteen levels of office space including the Mezzanine level located between the first and second floors. The CEO's office was located on the twelfth floor, as well as two other executive offices, the Board of Directors Room, the Law Library, a kitchen and a dining room. A smaller top level was used for the building utilities.

When Honor started work at Edison she worked on the Mezzanine level. She said she opted to take the stairs from the ground level to the Mezanine for the exercise rather than an elevator for just one level. Later, as she rose up the career ladder, she took the elevator to the eleventh and twelfth floors.

# Chapter 12 – Life in the Office

WHEN HONOR FIRST STARTED at Edison, it was 1946 and life in the office was devoid of technology. All work was done at the office, not at home offices, or "Flex" time. The hours were 9 to 5 at a desk with a manual typewriter, carbon paper, typewriter eraser and "white-out;" they were were standard items at a stenographer's desk. There were manually operated adding machines and pencil sharpeners. You had to be proficient at Shorthand (a lost talent), penmanship using pen and blotters. Ball point pens didn't come into being until 1946.

There were "Ditto" and "Mimeograph" copy machines, "Dictaphones," "dial telephones" and Intra-office "Intercom" and a phone for communications with all Edison facilities. They depended on "Information" and "Long distance operators." Outside telephone calls went through a switchboard. Written communication was sent by messengers and office boys. telegram and Postal Service "Snail Mail." There were no "FAX" machines then.

Today's secretary would be lost without a computer, printer, keyboard, or "shredder."

There were no Cell phones, "Face Book," E-Mail, or Word Processors; no UPS, US Postal or FedEX package delivery service; no electric typewriters, calculators or pencil sharpeners; no message answering machines, "Call Waiting," "Caller I.D," telephone Area Codes, or "911."

In addition to recording everything, you had to be the boss's receptionist and a buffer between the boss and unwanted callers. Honor routinely dealt with the boss's contemporaries, friends and favor-seekers. Honor received a call from Ronald Reagan, California's past Governor, asking to speak with Mr. Horton (CEO). He wanted to know if Edison could direct him to a source to purchase utility poles that he could use at his ranch.

Actor Randolph Scott was one of Mr. Horton's golfing partners. Another of Mr. Horton' golfing partners was Mr. Terrell (Terry) Drinkwater, a member of the Edison Board of Directors and former CEO of Western Airlines. He was a golfing partner of Dodger broadcaster Vin Scully. He arranged for Honor to meet Vin, for whom she had great admiration, being an avid Dodger fan.

An office dress code for men was suits with ties; for the ladies, it was dresses or dress suits. When "Pant-Suits" came into vogue, some secretaries asked if they could wear them to the office. They were told that when Honor Muller started wearing pant suits, they could too. In time pant suits became appropriate office attire. Of course the type of operations out in the field dictated the field work attire.

*During my 40 year career at Edison I met many very fine people, including all my bosses and co-workers. Close friendships were forged, and I am still in touch with many of those people at this writing in 2016, even though "geography" has spread us far apart and time has taken its toll.*

*Telephone calls and Emails keep us connected. The list is too long, to include everyone I knew.*

*I've chosen six of my close friends and co-workers to describe. I want to mention someone I met during my first week of employment. His name is* **Harold Kelley***. Harold and I were both 18 years old in 1946 when we started at Edison in entry level positions. Harold was a Draftsman and I was a Stenographer. We both moved up the ladder over the years to retirement. We keep in touch by telephone calls, reminiscing about our "adventures" during our long tenure at Edison and we marvel at our 70-year friendship.*

*Harold is married to Marilyn, a fellow Executive Secretary and friend. They often get together for lunch with fellow Edison retirees who reside in the Southern California area, fairly close to the relocated Edison Corporate Offices in Rosemead, California where we worked. Harold often calls me after these get-togethers to update me. No one, except 3 of my nieces, has known me for that long.*

**George Hanawalt, District Manager.** *I met George Hanawalt in the early years of my Edison career. We both worked in the Industrial Relations Department at the time the Company's two unions called a strike against Management. This required many extra hours of work for many employees in our department. George was our leader and "coach" and managed to keep us all focused, as well as "cheering" our group on as we continued to be productive. He was a mentor for me when I was faced with some decisions involving career direction. After his retirement and move to New Mexico to undertake a "career" in farming, Len and I enjoyed a reunion on one of our trips in the Southwest.*

***Kathy (Howard) Allen*** *joined Edison in 1951 as Secretary to Mr. William Mullendore, the President and CEO of the Company. I had applied for that position during the period that I was in the Executive Department performing duties as an "extra" secretary. I was told that it was to be filled by someone from outside the Company. I wasn't unduly upset about this as I was soon selected to be secretary to a Vice President, Mr. Kenyon. This was the perfect outcome on two levels: my experience working as Mr. Kenyon's secretary was an invaluable career opportunity for me. Kathy and I became "best friends." Over the years we took vacations together and enjoyed many social outings together.*

*Her parents, Ruth and Perry Howard, became special friends, as well as an extention of my family. I lived wth the Howards for almost five years. Kathy married Reid Allen in 1959. I was her "Maid of Honor." Kathy and Reid live in Pasadena. We now keep in touch by telephone. We treasure our long and special friendship, which came about because of our Edison connection.*

***Marie Tyerman*** *joined Edison in 1956 as a Kitchen Designer in the Marketing Department. Edison was promoting "All Electric Living" offering free services to customers in designing kitchens with electric stoves and cooktops. We became friends and enjoyed many social outings together in the form of eating out, seeing movies and plays, as well as vacations and an occasional weekend trip to San Francisco. Our friendship has been a lasting one. Marie is now living in a retirement care center in Southern California. We keep in touch by telephone calls.*

*Another significant worker was **Mary (Poulos) Doufas**. She was secretary to the Corporate Secretary. I had the opportunity of working with her when I was secretary to Mr. Horton, the CEO.*

*I was well aware of her efficiency and the quality of the work that she performed, working closely with her in preparation of Board Of Directors meetings and related documents. When I became Corporate Secretary, I "inherited" Mary as my secretary and "right arm." She made the transition so much smoother for me. We had a perfect working relationship. We became very close friends, as well. We kept in touch after my retirement, getting together socially with her and her husband, John. Sadly, Mary succumbed to her battle against cancer and is missed by all who knew her.*

**Vilma Sinclair**, secretary to the Director of Execuive Development, became a co-worker somewhat by "accident." Her boss, Russ Adams, and Vilma were relocated to space in the "Executive Suite" for a short duration while their office underwent reconfiguration. Her desk was close to mine and I wantd to make her feel comfortable in a "zone" she had considered somewhat "formidable." She was soon at ease in her new environment. During the next few months we developed a friendship sharing our mutual interests in books and music. Our friendship continued after my retirement. We still stay connected by eMails and telephone calls. She often commented that if it had not been for her temporary office relocation, I would still be known to her as secretary to the CEO, just someone to say"Hi" to without becoming a friend.

After my husband Len's death in 1999, I received many phone calls and notes of condolences from my former co-workers at Edison who had seen the notice of Len's "Memoriam" in the EDISON NEWS, our "house organ." Most of the callers were co-workers I had not seen since my retirement. It made me realize that our Company was "extended family" in this sense.

## Chapter 13 – The Hierarchy

*My first boss for the first two and a half years was **Leonard Muller**, manager of office administration.*

***Gilbert Woodman** was my boss for the next year. He was Superintendent of the Hydro Division.*

*By the time I had reached the age of twenty-one I was moved up to the Executive Department where I was secretary to **Noel B. Hinson**, Vice President and Executive Engineer.*

*Following Mr. Hinson's retirement I became secretary to **Raymond G. Kenyon**, Vice-President of Industrial Relations. The assignment lasted for three and a half years from 1951 to 1954. During this period, the Southern California Edison Company endured a labor strike. As a salaried member of Mr. Kenyon's staff, I continued to work with him until the strike was settled.*

*My next opportunity for a step up the ladder came when President and CEO, **Harold Quinton,** offered me the opportunity of a promotion to the position as his second secretary.*

*In 1958, I completed a one year Program in Business Administration, co-sponsored by Radcliffe College and Harvard Business School at Cambridge, MA. I returned to Edison and assumed my new duties as Secretary to the new President, **Jack K. Horton,** until I was elected Corporate Secretary in 1979.*

# The Fourth Rung
## Self Improvement

# Chapter 14 – Harvard Business School

*After working ten years at Southern California Edison Company (SCEC). in Los Angeles, I took a one-year leave of absence to attend a special Program in Business Administration, co-sponsored by Radcliffe College and Harvard Business School. This was a one-year program in Business Administration, designed specifically for women to give them a "running start" in the world of business. Classes were held in Radcliffe Collge, Cambridge, MA, and taught by Harvard Business School professors. The leave of absence was without any payment of salary by Edison, nor any contribution to this course of study.*

*I was the only woman in the class without an under-graduate degree. At the end of the school year we were awarded a Certificate in Business Administration.*

*I learned about the program from Ted Hermann, a former employer of my sister, Margaret (aka- Mickey). He had attended a special course for high level management people at the Harvard Business School. He sent me a brochure of the program for women, with the thought that Edison Co. would sponsor me. I had known that would not happen, but it generated my interest enough that I was determined to take the leave and pay for the course myself.*

*My mother had died, March 21, 1958, while I was away, and I was not sure whether I would return to Edison, or seek another employer at some other location. Mr. Harold Quinton, then CEO of Edison, was in Boston for an industry association meeting and asked me to be his guest for dinner, as he wanted to discuss my plans for my future. He then told me about Edison's plan to bring a PG&E (Pacific Gas and Electric) executive to Edison at the level of Executive Vice President with the view of becoming the next CEO. He suggested that it would be a "good fit" for both of us since I knew the personnel, which would be helpful to a "newcomer." I accepted the offer to become secretary to this person, although he could not disclose his name at that time.*

*I completed my course of study at Radcliffe College in 1958. I visited family and friends before returning to California where I lived with my close friends, the Howards. Kathy Howard was my best friend and her parents were like an aunt and uncle to me. They had a large home in Los Angeles in an area close to downtown.*

*After a short vacation I reported back to work for Mr. Quinton. I assumed my new duties as secretary to Mr.* **Jack K. Horton** *the following February, 1959. I worked for him for the next twenty years until I was elected Corporate Secretary in 1979. I continued to handle his secretarial needs on a part-time basis until my retirement, January 1, 1987, having completed 40 years of service with the Edison Company.*

It took courage to up, and take a one year leave of absence, without pay, scholarship, or company support. Of course, she had no college experience and a year at Harvard would give her increased credibility, qualification, and gain respect in her quest to fulfill her career goal.

Fig. 17 – Jack Horton

Quinton's successor was **Jack Horton.** He was a "Mover and Shaker." I would be remiss if I did not include a story of a man's rise to the top of the ladder; besides, he was Honor's boss for the next 20 years to the end of 1979 and very important in her life. He was a lad of modest means. Of course , there is little comparison between Honor's and Mr. Horton's rise in the business world; Honor had to start from scratch. It was a man's world and there was a "Glass Ceiling" that women had to penetrate.

Honor had a copy of his autobiography among her papers, titled "MY LIFE." Horton's children, considering his outstanding career, wanted him to write his autobiography. He showed it to her and asked her what she thought; she said, "It's too short." This is a condensed version:

He was born in Stanton, Nebraska in June, 1916. His father died when he was two years old. He and his brother were raised by his grandparents. His grandfather was President of the Bank in Orchard, Nebraska. Back then, there was no State or Federal regulation of banks, to speak of.

His environment fostered his education to such an extent, that he skipped the second grade, and fifth, as well. From then on, his new contemporaries had been two years older than he. He graduated from high school at age 15. He took off for Stanford with $25.00 in his pockiet. His mother had received a modest inheritance from his grandparents' estate allowing her to pay his college fees of $25.00 per school quarter. He was able to find part-time employment to supplement his limited income.

With the help of the Dean of Men at Stanford, his first job was with Shell Oil Company. He married Betty Magee, his "girl friend" from Lincoln, Nebraska, in 1937. He went to Law School at night and passed the California Bar Exam in 1940. He became a Legislatiive Representative initially, with the intent to open his own law office; however, WWII came and changed the direction of his career. He had wanted to join the Navy, but was rejected because he could not pass the eye test. He expected to be drafted but was not.

His next employer was Standard Oil Company representing the company in negotiating a significnt contract dispute between Standard Oil and the Navy. The CEO of Standard Oil then offered him the job as President of Pacific Public Service Company (PPS), a holding company for subsidiaries in gas, electric and water and pipeline businesses. PPS sold its interests to Pacific Gas and Electric

Company; he joined PG&E as a Vice President. His principal job there was to establish a pipeline for transporting natural gas from Alberta, Canada across British Columbia to the U.S. In the process, he became acquainted personnally with the Premiers of both Provinces. The family moved to Alberta, and the children enjoyed the new experience of sledding in the snow, but found the winter lasted too long.

About this time in mid-winter, with temperature dropping to minus 34 degrees F., he received a telephone call from Harold Quinton, then CEO of Edison Company, offering him the position of Executive Vice President. He responded that he currently held the comparable position at PG&E and would not make the move for that position. Following that discussion Mr. Quinton met with the Executive Committee of the Board of Directors, proposing that Edison bring Jack Horton in as President and that he, Quinton, move up to the position of Chairman of the Board and remain CEO. (While the Executive Committee was deliberating that option, Mr. Horton dictated his resume' to Honor, who was still the second secretary in Mr. Quinton's office.) This option was approved unanimously. Beginning February 1, 1959, Honor assumed the job as secretary to the new President, Jack Horton. He became CEO in 1965.

An early and difficult challenge involved a proposed Federal high-voltage electric transmission line extending from Canada to Southern California. This was vigorously opposed by Edison and other California investor owned utilities because it would compete with their existing lines. Mr. Horton testified before Congress as well as the California Legislature. The utilities' position prevailed.

During Nixon's Presidency, Nixon offered Horton a Cabinet post as Secretary of Energy, the first "Energy Czar." That meant leaving Edison Company and moving to Washington, D.C.. When he discussed it with his wife, she made it clear that, "If you accept, you will be going alone." That, of course, ended that.

The Hortons also had a social connection with President Nixon. They were invited to the White House on more than one occasion to enjoy dinner and an evening of entertainment, including special artists, as well as entertainers from Broadway musicals.

# Chapter 15 – Social Life

## Church

### Hollywood Presbyterian Church

*My "Faith Journey" began in Hudson, New York, where our family attended the Presbyterian Church. My sister Mickey and I sang in the church choir of about a dozen people, with mostly "average" voices. Our choir director was also the music director of our high school. Mickey and I sang in the school A Capella Choir and the Girl's Glee Club.*

*We also attended a young people's group called "Christian Endeavor;" not characterized as a Sunday School class. This group met at church late Sunday afternoon, followed by some of us going to the local grill for coffee and conversation. The appeal of this gathering was probably "It's where the boys are."*

*When we moved to California, we attended "Hollywood Presbyterian Church." It was here that my faith journey became meaningful. Dr. Louis Evans was the Senior Pastor and a marvelous preacher. Many people from the entertainment field worshipped there, including actors Dennis Morgan, Jane Russell, Virginia Mayo, Colleen Townsend and singer Connie Haines.*

*There was a Sunday School class called "College Department" for college age and young working people. Dr. Henrietta Mears was the leader. She, truly, was a "force." She made the Bible come alive; it was obvious that she lived her strong faith. She also had a wonderful sense of humor. Her classes on Sunday morning and Wednesday evening were packed. Several young men went on to become ministers, due to her nurturing.*

*My sister met her future husband, Spencer Nilson, in this environment. They were married in the Chapel of this church. Spencer had a very good bass voice and sang in the Cathedral Choir. The choir had about 50 members. The choir had a paid Quartet; Harve Presnell was the tenor. He became a celebrity in films and Broadway Musicals. The music director, Dr. Charles Hirt, was also the head of the Music Department of the University of California (USC). The Number two choir was called the "Chancel Choir;" they sang for Sunday evening service. I joined this group and sang in the Alto section; Mickey sang in the Soprano section. On occasion, we substituted for the Cathedral Choir.*

## Bel Air Presbyterian Church

*Mickey and I met Louis Evans, Jr., (Dr. Evans' son) and Colleen "Coke" Townsend in the College Department of the Hollywood Presbyterian Church. Coke was an actress then, making films at 20th Century Fox Studio. Lou and Coke were in love and were married. Coke resigned as an actress and joined Lou while he was finishing Seminary at San Anselmo, CA. Since Coke was a promising young actress, this was duly noted by the "Tabloids" of the time, speculating that this marriage probably would not last when she realized that she had given up what appeared to be a great career as an actress. (Of course, the speculators were all wrong, and the marriage thrived, lasting until Lou's death, 58 years later.)*

*Upon being ordained as a Presbyterian minister, Lou was called to form a new church, which was designated, Bel Air Presbyterian Church. Many of us, who had known Lou and Coke for many years, transferred our "Letter" (Membership) to join the young Bel Air Church. Initially, meetings were held in their home, and Sunday Services were held at Bel Air Elementary School until the church facility was built. Mickey and Spencer Nilson were among the "Founding Members." Spencer was an "Elder" and Mickey was in charge of the "start-up" of the Sunday School Program.*

*After returning home to California in 1958 from my Business School Year at Radcliffe, I became active in church activities. I taught Sunday School at the Primary level. During that time Carrie Fisher and her brother, Todd, attended the class for a short time. Ronald Reagan and Nancy attended church services on a regular basis. At that time, he was Governor of California. After becoming President of the U.S. , their attendance became infrequent due to the "distraction" his Security issues created.*

*Donn Moomaw, then the Senior Pastor of Bel Air Church offered the Invocation Prayer at each of President Reagan's Inaugural Ceremonies. Moomaw had been a successful professional football player with the L.A. Rams team until he decided that football would not be his career. He felt a "Calling" to become a full time Christian minister.*

## Friends

Honor was not "all work and no play," up until Len became "an item." The only serious attachment she had experienced was with Harvard Business School student Jay Dunn while she was in Boston in 1957 - 58.

*Jay introduced me to professional baseball. He was an avid "New York Yankees fan." He suggested that since the Dodgers were moving from Brooklyn to Los Angeles that summer (1958), I would have a great opportunity to see some good baseball games, and might even become a Dodgers "fan." He suggested that I get a foretaste of the game: thus, we attended a Yankee vs. Boston Red Sox game at the famous Fenway Park in Boston. During the summer we attended a couple games at Yankee Stadium in New York City before I returned home to Los Angeles. (As it turned out, I did indeed become an avid and loyal fan of the Dodgers).*

*Jay, and his good friend, Ken, taught me how to water-ski during the summer of 1958. Ken's parents had a summer home at one of the many lakes in New Jersey.*

*The following year we exchanged letters and phone calls, but they became fewer and fewer. Jay planned to make a trip to Los Angeles, accompanied by his friend Ken, to see me, as well as do some sight-seeing. However I had a letter from Jay saying that he could not justify the cost of the trip for just one week's vacation. He asked how I felt about making a trip east to see him, and give us a chance to talk about our continuing relationship. I wrote back, indicating that I felt his letter contained a real message about our relationship; essentially, that it was time to end it. He telephoned me when he received my letter. We both agreed that long-distance relationships rarely succeed. No heartbreak on either side.*

*I saw Jay two or three times after that, when he was in Los Angeles on business. He had married and had two children. He telephoned me in 1963 when he learned, through a mutual friend, that I was engaged to be married. He wished me well, and that was our final communication.*

# Chapter 16 – Len Muller - Biography

HONOR WAS NOT anti-social, by any means. She dated co-workers, but did not encourage any lasting relationships; that is, until Len Muller entered the picture, two years after he had become a widower. Remember, Len was the one who hired her as a stenographer in his department in 1946.

Fig. 18 - Len Muller

Leonard Muller spent some forty-five years of his life working for Southern California Edison. It wasn't until he retired at the age of sixty-five, that he began to paint. Born in San Francisco, he spent his early years in Madera. He lived in Monrovia while attending high school and Pasadena City College. In 1930, he began working at SCEC. He continued there while he completed his education at UCLA, graduating with a degree in Business Administration in 1934.

He remembered receiving fundamental art instruction in high school, but, it was not until retirement that he began thinking about developing his skills as an artist. "You go stale sitting at home." he said of retirement. "I have to have something to occupy my time; so, I took up painting."

He returned to Pasadena City College where he spent two years drawing and painting while studying under a well known artist, Robert Uecker. He developed a special interest in the techniques of water color. His subjects included scenes that he had photographed during his extensive travels. Some of his paintings were displayed at the historic Pasadena Playhouse.

He was a prolific painter. When he had accumulated most of his work, he had a formal "showing." Honor, still working, was one of his earliest admirers. In fact, some of his paintings were hung in her office at the Edison Company when she became Corporate Secretary.

> *Since Len Muller was the person who hired me in 1946, we had known each other in the office environment over the years. Len folowed my progress with interest since he was the one who gave me my first job. Len's wife died in January 1962 while their son, Brian, was completing his college education at the Stanford University campus in Florence, Italy. In May of that year Len went to Europe to join Brian for a four week tour on the Continent in Brian's "Sunbeam" automobile, a graduation gift from his grandfather.*
>
> *One day in May 1963, I was waiting at a signal to cross the street when Len approached.*
>
> *While exchanging pleasantries, I mentioned my upcoming trip to Spain and Italy with my cousin Dorothy Dohrmann. He showed some interest since he and Brian had spent some time in touring Italy. As we went our separate ways, he commented that he would like to hear more about my trip. The next evening he telephoned me, inviting me to dinner, indicating he would be interested in my itinerary.*
>
> *We had a delightful evening. He shared some of his experiences visiting many of the locations on my itinerary.*
>
> *We had one more dinner date and two lunch get-togethers before I left on May 30, to be gone for four weeks. At each hotel, when Dorothy and I checked in, the hotel clerk would say, as he handed us our keys, "Miss Moore, a letter for you." There was always a letter from Len waiting for me at every location. After about a week of this, Dorothy commented, "Should I be making airline reservations to attend a wedding in Los Angeles?" (Dorothy lived in Brooklyn, New York.)*
>
> *I commented, "Not so fast!"*

*When I returned from the trip, Len was there to meet me, along with my sister Mickey, my nephew Spencer Evan and my niece Lisa Nilson. Mickey mentioned later that she noticed, after I was greeted with hugs and kisses from Mickey's two children, that Len was next in line for the "welcome home" hug!*

*We dated from then on and enjoyed "getting to know you" on a social level, although we had known each other for seventeen years. We both felt very comfortable in each other's company. Over time, we got to meet each other's family members. It seemed that there was unanimous approval on both sides. Our respective friends also seemed to approve of this match.*

*When Len proposed marriage and I had said "yes," he suggested a Christmas wedding. It was tempting, but on a practical side, I had no vacation time left for that year and, in fact, I had taken an extra week without pay, for my trip.*

# Chapter 17 – Marriage -1964

*In 1963 I had moved from the Howard's home to a furnished apartment in Los Angeles. I lived in the apartment until Len and I were married. We arranged to be married on February 8, 1964, the closest date to Valentine's Day available at my church. We were married at the Bel Air Presbyterian Church on Saturday, February 8, 1964 at 4:00 p.m.. Mickey was my "matron of honor" and Lisa, my niece, was our winsome "flower girl." A Reception followed in the Fellowship Hall of the church. We went to Hawaii for our two week "honeymoon."*

Fig. 19 - Honor and Len - wedding

# Chapter 18 – Life Out of The Office

ONE OF THE ADVANTAGES of living in Los Angeles during our working years was the proximity to activities we enjoyed. The Music Center in downtown Los Angeles was only five miles from our home. The center had three separate theater buildings; the Dorothy Chandler Pavilion, Ahmanson Theater and the Mark Taper Forum. Operas and Broadway musicals, as well as single artist performances, were held at the Dorothy Chandler Pavilion, the largest of the three theater units. The Ahmanson Theater was the the setting for plays. The Mark Taper Forum was the smallest of the three. It had a "thrust" stage. This was the smallest, with the audience "wrapping" around a portion of the stage.

If a theater-goer was sitting in the front row, he or she, could expect some "moisture" as the actors emoted. We enjoyed the opportunity to hear beautiful music, and great drama, as well.

The Dorothy Chandler Pavilion had an "upscale" dining room a the top level of the building. The food was excellent and the view of the city lights at night was an added treat. In the early 1970's the annual Oscar Awards presentations were held there a few times.

During the summer months we enjoyed attending performances at the Hollywood Bowl, including symphonies and "Pop" music. One evening we were guests of friends of ours who had seats very close to the stage. This was a great location to fully appreciate the music of Duke Ellington and his band and Ella Fitzgerald. The Greek Theater, located in near-by Griffith Park, also provided summer entertainment. This was where we saw "The Carpenters" perform as an opening act before the featured entertainer, Andy Williams, took the stage that evening.

We enjoyed films and there was no shortage of movie theaters. The famous Graumann's Chinese Theater was very popular, especially for the tourists to see the hand and footprints of the movie stars pressed into the cement in front of the theater. The ornateness of the décor, both inside and outside, was an added attraction. An added incentive for seeing a movie at Graumann's was its next *door neighbor, C.C.Brown's Old Fashioned Ice Cream Parlor. This was a family owned operation renowned for its hot fudge sauce.*

*Westwood (home to UCLA) had a concentration of movie houses along with many restaurants offering a variety of menus. Also, there were a number of theaters in the area showing foreign films. There was no shortage of choices for entertainment.*

*We both liked to read so we took advantage of the Los Angeles Public Library on a regular basis. Suspense and mystery writers were among our favorites. Our TV viewing focused mainly on Public Broadcasting System (PBS) TV programs. Masterpiece Theater on Sunday evenings, provided quality entertainment. In particular, we enjoyed watching episodes of "The Forsyth Saga" and "Upstairs- Downstairs ," and many more. Thursday evenings featured mystery series, like "Prime Suspect" with Helen Mirren. We watched the McNeal-Lehrer Report, the nightly news program.*

*Our respective families lived in the Southern California area and we enjoyed many get-togethers for dinner and entertainment. Also, Len had a set of friends he had known from the early days of his marriage. I had many friends, as well, and of course, we both had our Edison friends.*

*We enjoyed dining out. We were fortunate to have a limitless choice of restaurants for fine dining. We had our favorites; French food topped the list as our first choice, but, we also enjoyed Mexican and the many other ethnic foods. When we just wanted a bite, we settled for a hamburger.*

*When we ate at home, Len and I did the cooking together. We liked to cook as a team. After Len's retirement, he took over the cooking duties on week days. After I retired we resumed sharing the kitchen duties. We liked to entertain and we liked trying out new recipes. I always enjoyed setting the table for "company" using special table settings and candles. We enjoyed a very active and satisfying, "Life Out Of The Office."*

## Travels Abroad With Len

One of the perks of Honor's "longevity" at Edison was a paid three-week vacation. Her first trip abroad was with her cousin Dorothy Dohrmann in 1963 (Trip #1), the year before she and Len were married. She had taken an additional week without pay, allowing ample time to enjoy "first trip" adventures. These included a bull-fight in Madrid, viewing exquisite art at the Prado and many other well-known museums in Spain, Italy and France. A bus trip from the French Riviera, traveling along the Italian Riviera to Portofino, Italy was a memorable highlight of "first trip" impressions.

This whetted her appetite for foreign travel, resulting in eighteen trips abroad. Honor kept a journal for each of the trips, recording in detail the memorable sights, adventures in meeting new people, and sampling the cuisine and wine of the countries visited. Her detailed notes provided a "history" to be enjoyed over time as a remembrance of special vacations; they also served as useful reference to recommend favorite hotels and restaurants to friends.

I have read each of Honor's 18 journals, which I found to be immensely interesting, as well as educational. Although this significant aspect of her life would be of interest, I think, to the readers of this book, it would be impractical to include, as such Travelogue would cover almost 800 pages of her own notes. However, some "highlights" of notable trips will be shared – "in her own words …."

## Travel Abroad with Cousin Dorothy Dohrmann
### Trip #1

Trip #1 – SPAIN, ITALY and FRANCE - (Madrid, Rome, Paris, Portofino and Monaco) - 1963

## Travels Abroad with Len
### Trips #2 thru #18 - September 11, 1965 to September 17, 1998

Trip #2 – HOLLAND, ENGLAND, GERMANY. AUSTRIA, BELGIUM and FRANCE. - 1965

Tr1p #3 – DENMARK, YUGOSLAVIA, GREECE, AUSTRIA and SPAIN (Cruise Greek Islands) - 1967

Trip #4 – HOLLAND, ENGLAND and WALES (London and Cornwall area) - 1968

Trip #5 – DENMARK, SWEDEN, SWITZERLAND, AUSTRIA, GERMANY and ENGLAND - 1970

Trip #6 – FRANCE, SPAIN, SWITZERLAND and DENMARK -1972

Trip #7 – SPAIN - (Prado Museum, Plain of La Mancha and Valley of the Fallen) - 1973

Trip #8 – ENGLAND (Canal Trip) and SCOTLAND - 1975

Trip #9 – HOLLAND, SWEDEN, FINLAND, USSR (In-tourist - Iron Curtain) and POLAND - 1976

Trip #10 – ENGLAND AND SCOTLAND (Hampshire, Cornwall to Edinburgh) - 1977

Trip #11 – SPAIN, FRANCE and MONTE CARLO. (Nice and Cannes) - 1979

Trip #12 – ENGLAND and EGYPT (Up the Nile) - 1981

Trip #13 – ENGLAND - 1983 (Visit Brit friends, Rector of Coberley and Canterbury)

Trip #14 – DENMARK, AUSTRIA (Vienna Opera "La Traviata") FRANCE and ENGLAND - 1985

Trip #15 – ZURICH, FRANCE, GENEVA and ENGLAND - 1987

Trip #16 – IRELAND and ENGLAND (Dublin, Guinness factory, Countys Kerry and Clare - 1993

Trip #17 – LONDON HOLIDAY (London plays, Piccadilly, Shepherd's Market ,Grenwich Clock) -1994

Trip #18 – PRAGUE to PASSAU, GERMANY - (Danube Culture tour.) - 1998

All of Honor's trips abroad were fun, challenging and educational. During the sixties and seventies, travel arrangements were simpler. Extreme security measures were unneeded; consquently, they were free to come and go at will. The only delays were related to air travel, money changing and border crossings.

She and Len explored the museums, churches and galleries. They toured the great cities of Europe and historical sites by land, sea and air; by car, bus, train, cruise ship, on foot and on camel and donkey; but, mostly by rental car.

They learned about local customs and they sampled the foods of each nationality. Honor enjoys cooking, so she was very interested in what was on the menu. I would describe her as a "Foodie." The proof is written in her Trip Logs where half of every page has to do with restaurants and the food that was served at every stop. I know, I am the lucky recipient of her "Candlelight Suppers" and an occasional, formal dinner for guests.

# Honor's Travels

*Len and I made our first trip to Europe in 1965 (Trip #2). We took delivery of our Jaguar at the Jaguar agency showroom in the heart of London. The purchase had been made through the Jaguar agency in Los Angeles, as well as the arrangements for shipping the car home to Los Angeles. We drove 3300 miles on the Continent before delivering the car to Antwerp, Belgium for its "boat ride" to the port of Los Angeles. Driving a left-hand drive automobile in the London traffic was "memorable," and we were grateful to arrive safely at Dover, after successfully navigating many miles driving on the "wrong side" of the road. It was a great relief to board the ferry for the trip across the English Channel to Calais, France. It was special to tour the countries in our own vehicle instead of a rental car.*

*Our next trip in 1967 (Trip #3) took us to a part of the world we knew only from history books – Greece, the "cradle of our civilization." The highlight of this trip was a 7-day cruise on the Aegean Sea, visiting the Greek Islands – each one fascinating with its own place in history. A tour of Athens and its environs made ancient history come alive. We also visited Dubrovnik, Yugoslavia, including a guided tour of the Dalmatian Coast. We were introduced to Slivovitz, a popular Croatian brandy drink. It is not unlike Ouzo, a Greek liqueur, in terms of its punch. We found that "less is more" on a hot afternoon drive over curving coastal roads. Our driver/guide showed us a beautiful secluded beach, suggesting we could go "skinny dipping" to cool off. Tempting, but we opted to wait until we returned to our hotel and don our swim wear. Our hotel was located right at the water's edge; the plunge into the cool water was life-giving.*

*To celebrate Len's retirement from Edison in 1975 (Trip #8) we joined Len's sister and brother-in-law, Marion and Lotie Smith, plus two of their long-time friends, Lois and Joe Sprankle, to share a unique experience. We rented a canal boat to ply the Shropshire and Llangollen Canals in England/Wales. Our long, narrow boat was named "Juliet," our home for the next six days. We had opened and closed more than sixty locks and drawbridges during the trip.*

*Due to rain and cold weather, an ersatz shower, plus a "head" that didn't work, our "crew" unanimously voted to stay at a real hotel in Llangollen, Wales about midway through the trip. The amenities of the hotel revived us to enjoy more laughs and experiences as we returned to our starting "port." A chapter could be devoted to the various incidents we experienced during this short "cruise." However, I think the following limerick, composed by Lotie Smith, sums it all up and continues to make us smile in remembrance.*

## ODE TO THE 'JULIET'

*Here's to the "Juliet" – a sturdy little craft, designed like a "collier" – steel fore and aft.*
*Midst light-hearted laughter, we took in our lines and set our course through wild blackberry vines, and emerald field, mighty oaks and chestnut trees that lined our way from Waverton to Dees.*

*With our quarter dozen captains we all laughed. We have a date with destiny in our sturdy little craft.*

*There were sheep and cows and horses and tawny colored hogs.*
*There were swans and ducks and geese and a spate of friendly dogs.*
*There were dour, phlegmatic fishermen and "googies" and eels, and the ever-present pensioners eating picnic meals.*

*There was a "head" that really did not work. There was a midnight misadventure into the town of Chirk.*

*There were freezing morning watches – a couple in the rain; and a rustic little shower, but none were quite so vain.*
*There were endless locks and bridges for willing hands to tend.*
*There were hidden bars and ridges for the captain's hand to fend.*

*Every trip must have its hang-up – ours was in a lock.*
*The captain was at the tiller; the crew was on the dock.*
*Our bow was in the water; our stern was in the air.*
*The cook was in the galley, tearing out her hair.*
*Then suddenly it was over, with a roller coaster splash*

*that sent us bounding forward to a steel-plated crash.*
*If you want to be a sailor, and are a little daft,*
*Take on the mighty "Juliet" – a sturdy little craft.*

*In the summer of 1976 (Trip #9) we embarked on another air/sea adventure, starting in Scandinavia. The M.T.S. Daphne was our "home at sea" for the next fourteen days, with ports of call in Norway, Sweden, Denmark, Finland and Poland. The highlight was our brief visit to Leningrad (now known as St. Petersburg, U.S.S.R.) The night before arriving at port we had a lecture as to procedures and what we could expect as "guests" touring Leningrad. We were aware of searchlights playing on our ship from small patrol boats. A member of the Daphne's staff commented that they always knew when they entered Russian waters when the patrol boats "welcomed" the ship to port.*

*The following morning we lined up to board the busses to take us to the Hermitage Museum. Before departing the ship we were "processed" by the dour soldiers who took our Passports and Visas. The Visa was a document valid for this visit only, then turned in to our "host" country at the end of our visit. Our Passports were in their custody until the morning we departed the port.*

*It was a gloomy, rainy Sunday, matching the faces of most of the people we encountered, except for Nina, our pleasant guide and docent for that day's tour. The Hermitage is huge, containing paintings by the famous European artists, as well as magnificent tapestries. Nina pointed out a Goya portrait, which was a gift to the Hermitage from Armand Hammer, a well-known Los Angeles, CA art collector and philanthropist.*

*The Museum was packed with people, making it difficult for Nina to corral our group, and for us to follow her, as well. Nina explained the reason for such a crowd. The Russian people have free admission to the Museum on Sunday. Since the weather was so unpleasant, the locals could not enjoy their usual picnics and outdoor entertainment, thus chose shelter at the Museum. She commented: "I wish it were not so on this day of your visit." We all shared her wish. We would have liked to be able to return the next day for a more leisurely viewing of the contents. However, that was not possible as we were "Intourist" visitors and our activities were conducted with their selected guides.*

*Another "Intourist" event on our agenda was a program of Armenian Folk Dancing – an excellent performance. When we were seated in the theater, we realized the audience was comprised of tourists from many countries. This was another "Intourist" venue where Russians are not allowed to enter; as tourists, we could not attend an event at a Russian theater.*

*The Russian soldiers were posted at our ship during our entire stay. Our Passports were returned to us the morning we departed – a good feeling to take possession of this important document.*

*The Daphne was required to fly the Russian flag while we were in port; thus. great joy to see the American flag in its rightful place.*

*A Russian pilot took the Daphne out of the channel and was with us for the next two hours. He was an older man and did not look so stern and "militarized" as our guards. Some of us waved to him while he was on the bridge; he nodded and returned the wave. We watched him as he descended the "Jacob's Ladder" to board the Pilot boat. We called "Goodbye" to him, and he acknowledged with a smile and a wave. This was a friendly "finale" to our brief taste of life, as we saw it, behind the "Iron Curtain."*

"You can't appreciate Home, until you've left it;
… Nor 'Old Glory', 'til you see it hanging on a broomstick
on the Shanty of a Consul in a foreign town."
– O. Henry

*In the Fall of 1981 (Trip #12) Len and I embarked on an adventure to a different Continent – Africa. We signed up with Lindblad Travel for a trip to Egypt. Our tour started in London with an introduction to an important segment of Egyptian history. The British Museum housed many Egyptian artifacts and treasures of 5,000 years ago, including the Rosetta Stone, a significant part of Egyptology. This is a tablet inscribed with Greek and Egyptian hieroglyphics, and provides a key to deciphering these hieroglyphics. The Egyptologist, part of the Lindblad team, did a great job in providing some basic background before we embarked on our Nile adventure.*

*When we arrived at Cairo Airport, we were met by Valerie, our Hostess/ Guide for our stay in Egypt. She got us through baggage/customs procedures handily and on to the bus for transport to the Rameses Hilton, a very attractive new hotel on the Nile. Mr. and Mrs. Colman, Lindblad Managers for the Mideast area, were at the hotel to welcome us and assure us that Lindblad was making every effort to be certain we would be safe during our stay in Egypt.*

*NOTE; Egypt's President, Anwar Sadat, had been assassinated just two weeks before our trip. Some of our friends and family members had misgivings about our taking the trip at this time. Warren Christopher, former U.S. Secretary of State, was on the Board of Directors of Edison Company. Our Chairman of the Board asked him if we should consider canceling our trip. He assured me that if there was a major concern on the issue of travel in this region, our State Dept. would issue a warning to U.S. Travelers. On that basis, it was all "green lights" for our journey. We had been forewarned about the presence of soldiers at Cairo Airport, as well as on our route along the Nile, where some incidents had occurred shortly after the assassination. At these locations soldiers were on guard where our boat docked overnight. Fortunately, we did not experience any disruption during our trip.*

*While in Cairo, we visited the Mosques, the Great Pyramids at Ginza, and climbed 300 steps to the top of one of the most-visited pyramids for a spectacular view (and to be able to say we did it!) Of course, a camel ride is a "must," and an experience I do not plan to repeat. Valerie had given us some piasters (Egyptian money) to be used as "backsheesh" – tips for the camel drivers/escorts. She had cautioned us that the drivers would ask for US dollars instead, but do not give in to them; offer only the piasters. She also instructed us to tip after getting off the camel; otherwise, it would take more "backsheesh" to "disembark." Sure enough, Len's camel driver was persistent, wanting the "backsheesh" before lowering the camel; Len was equally adamant. It took one of the Egyptian guides to intervene, using language we were probably glad we did not understand, but it worked.*

*Our river boat, M.S. Pyramids, was somewhat spartan, compared to the more luxurious Sheraton boats we saw at Luxor. The Nile is shallow between Cairo and Luxor; thus, the larger boats are unable to navigate that portion of the Nile. "Simplicity" characterizes the nature of this craft, but adequate for all our needs. Our Egyptologist, Lotfi, was a gem. He made Egyptian history immensely interesting, had a great sense of humor, and an all-round delightful "shipmate." (Valerie told us that we were lucky to have drawn "the best" for our tour. She had done this Nile trip with others.)*

*A major highlight of the tour was visiting Luxor. Here we saw the tomb of King Tutankhamen and the Luxor Museum, housing some beautiful artifacts from King Tut's tomb.*

*The evening event was a very special experience. We attended a "Sound and Light" performance at the Temple of Karnak – an impressive display of lights and beautiful music. The finale – unscripted - the fall of a shooting star to conclude the drama.*

*A 30-minute flight from Aswan took us to Abu Simbel, where the rock-cut temples of King Rameses ll and his Queen Nefertiti were relocated when the High Dam at Aswan was built. ( The High Dam was funded by Russia; started in 1960 and completed in 1971.) The Temples are housed in an artificial mountain to re-create the original settings – an impressive engineering feat. The cost was approximately $40 million; the U.S. contributed $20 million.*

*Our final Nile experience was a sail on a felucca, an Egyptian sailboat propelled by sails or oars, if necessary. It was a beautiful afternoon with soft breezes, enabling us to sail to a small isle with a botanical garden. Lotfi was on our felucca and described some of the vegetation we saw.*

*He suggested we have a cup of tea with him at the end of the excursion. Len and I were so pleased to have this extra time with him before we went our separate ways. He shared photos and stories about his wife and family who live in Cairo.*

*And so back to Cairo for our last night before our flight to London the following day. The comfort and amenities of the Nile Hilton were welcome after two weeks of our boat accommodations. We joined "new" friends we had met on this journey to treat ourselves to a special dinner at an Arabesque restaurant Lotfi had recommended to us. After the simple fare on our boat, this was a gourmet delight and "finale" to another memorable trip.*

*Our last trip together was in September 1998 (Trip #18). Len's sister, Marion Smith, joined us for our "Storybook Musical Adventure." As suggested, music was the central theme of this journey, enjoyed in some famous opera houses, as well as concert halls in cities visited on our cruise on the Danube. It was an IST Cultural Tour River Cruise on the **MV Mozart.***

*Cruising on the Danube, we visited Durnstein and Vienna **(Austria)**, Esztergon, Szentendre and Budapest **(Hungary)**, Bratislavia **(Slovakia)**, Melk and Grein (Austria). On 10 September, we were treated to a private concert of Bartok's piano works, at the Bela Bartok Museum in Budapest.*

*Our IST Cultural Tours group met at Prague, Czech Republic, the starting point for our 10-day trip. Our three-some had arrived two days earlier to do some "exploring" on our own. The Palace Hotel was "first class" in every respect. When we arrived at the hotel, after experiencing flight delays and finding that our luggage had not arrived with us, our frustration was obvious. The Hotel Reception suggested we sit down in the attractive lobby, relax and enjoy a glass of champagne while they did some "tracking" for us. Of course, it all got sorted out, and when we returned to our rooms after a lovely dinner at the hotel, our luggage had been placed in our rooms.*

*The weather was perfect for our entire trip. We three enjoyed walking and taking in the "flavor" of this beautiful city, leaving the "must see" attractions for the scheduled tour.*

*A beautiful "Welcome" dinner, preceded by a champagne reception, provided a time to get acquainted with our fellow travelers and meet our IST guides for the trip. We enjoyed all the "official" sightseeing by bus and were glad we had the advantage of the guides.*

*We visited an old Jewish cemetery, and our stop there was very meaningful to Ruth, an elderly Jewish lady, traveling with her daughter, Lou. They located the graves of Ruth's grandparents. She had grown up in Prague, and as a young woman, attended operas at the Opera House, always in the SRO area. How special it was for her to now enjoy the operas from a very good seat in the Orchestra section. We attended two operas at the Prague Opera House. We were told by our IST hosts that the attendees at the opera "dressed up," suggesting we would probably be more comfortable doing the same. (We all did!) The Opera House was beautiful and the productions a special treat. Each night, following the opera, when we returned to the Hotel Palace, champagne and refreshments awaited us. (So civilized!)*

*We were taken by bus from Prague to Passau, Germany, where we boarded the M/V Mozart for our cruise on the Danube. The Mozart was a* neat "floating hotel," carrying 200 passengers. We were all delighted with the accommodations and amenities. We arrived in Vienna, Austria, after visiting various small cities in the Slovakia area. Another opera treat in Vienna – "La Traviata." Len and I had been to the magnificent Opera House before this trip and looked forward to a return visit.

Great memories of previous visits to Vienna, including some special restaurants and the devastating rich desserts. At Budapest, Hungary we had a special treat – a private concert at the Bela Bartok Museum. A most enjoyable afternoon listening to fine musicians. This was a special music finale event.

Len had his 88th birthday on September 10, while we were still aboard the Mozart. A surprise to Len and the rest of us at the end of our dinner. The lights dimmed and the waiters made a dramatic entrance with flaming Baked Alaska, adorned with candles, and 200 people sang "Happy Birthday" to Len. He looked at me, and I told him I was "innocent" – I had nothing to do with this surprise. Our Cultural Travels host then came to our table and told Len they had made note of his birth date from his Passport, and would not miss the opportunity to do something special. This was a birthday to remember, as well as a special "finale" for our Danube cruise.

We disembarked at Passau and were transported by bus to Munich Airport, where we all went our separate ways. Len, Marion and I went to London for a couple days before our return home.

This was our last travel adventure together, and we were so pleased that Marion could join us.

Charles has noted that I had 18 trips abroad. Although I have shared the highlights of selected trips, most all of our trips to Europe started or ended in London. We felt comfortable there because we could speak and mostly understand the language (excepting "cockney" and some others); and we always enjoyed going to the plays. Another important reason was to see our English friends in England.

We met a couple, Kathleen and Pat Barnett, through Mr. Horton's association with Borax Ltd., London. Mr. Horton was on the U.S. Borax Board of Directors, and made a trip to London for a special meeting. Arrangements for travel and other details were handled by communications between the two secretaries. Kathleen was secretary to Mr. Travis, CEO of Borax Ltd. After many *written and telephone conversations, Kathleen indicated she would like to meet us when we got to London again. That meeting occurred in the next few months, and it was the start of a warm and lasting friendship. Kathleen's husband, Pat, also worked for Borax. On our first meeting they met us at our hotel, took us to dinner and a play. (Borax treat!). We continued to see them each time we were in London, and were invited to their home in Sussex after they had retired. We were able to extend hospitality to Kathleen when she made a trip to Los Angeles in connection with Borax business. Our continuing friendship (exchange of Christmas cards and news) continued until Kathleen's death a few years ago.*

*We had the pleasure of meeting a delightful couple, Ian and Hilare Pulford of Coberley, England. This came about through Mr. William Coberly, a member of Edison's Board of Directors and my sister Mickey's employer. Mr. Coberly's "roots" were in Coberley, Eng.; thus his connection with Ian Pulford, the Rector of Coberley Church. Len and I visited the Cotswolds area many times, and Mr. Coberly suggested we meet the Pulfords who live in this area, and knew we would be warmly welcomed.*

*Such connection was made on our next trip to this area, and this was the genesis of a long and cherished friendship. Ian and his wife were very warm and hospitable. They always had a beautiful bouquet of flowers in our hotel room to greet and welcome us. We had the opportunity to reciprocate when they visited in Los Angeles. The Coberlys had gifted the Pulfords with a trip to CA for a visit. I had retired by that time, so Len and I were able to spend some time with them. We had a dinner at our home, inviting some of our friends to enjoy their company, as well.*

*Unfortunately, Ian Pulford had a stroke with crippling effects. He managed to continue as Rector for some time until he was disabled and retired. He had served his Parish for over 30 years and was beloved by all the neighboring communities. Fortunately, he had been honored with the title of Canon before the stroke limited his ability to serve. The Dean of St. Paul's Cathedral in London had participated in the ceremonies.*

"A Journey is a person in itself; no two are alike. And all plans, safeguards, policies and coercion are fruitless. We find after years of struggle that we do not take a trip, it takes us."

– JOHN STEINBECK

# Life Between Trips

*Honor and Len did have a life between trips. In 1967 they moved from their apartment in Los Angeles and purchased a home in Hollywood.*

*We lived in an apartment in Los Angeles for three years and in 1967 purchased a home in the Los Feliz/Hollywood Hills area of Los Angeles. ( In a neighborhood in close proximity to the famous "HOLLYWOOD" sign). This was an ideal location for us, with close access to the Hollywood Freeway for our daily commute to downtown Los Angeles. Our neighborhood bordered on the undeveloped area of Griffith Park, away from the hustle and bustle of urban living. Frequently we would see wildlife, such as deer and raccoons in our backyard. This was to become our home for the next 22 years.*

*We had enjoyed visiting Santa Barbara over the years of our marriage. We would often drive the 100 miles to have dinner at one of our all-time favorite restaurants returning home the same night. It had been a favorite weekend "get-away." We devoted a considerable amount of time checking out properties in Santa Barbara, but, never found the proper "fit" for us.*

*In 1974, a year before Len's retirement, we purchased a "town house" in Del Mar Woods, California. It was a housing development on the Pacific coast in North San Diego County. We enjoyed weekend "get-aways" and vacations there, having the beach virtually in our front yard. We had considered this as a possible future home for us after I had retired. However, the area experienced considerable expansion and growth in population. We realized that this would not be our choice for a retirement location. In the meantime family members enjoyed visiting the "Muller Beach House." Len's sister and brother- in-law (Marion and Lotie) and Len's cousin and his wife (Walt and Kay Muller) lived in the general area and we enjoyed many happy get-togethers with them when we were in residence at Del Mar Woods.*

# Chapter 19 – Dodgers' Fan

*I BECAME A DODGERS fan when the team moved from Brooklyn to Los Angeles. At the same time, I became a fan of Vin Scully. Vin Scully has been the "Voice of the Dodgers" since 1950, eight years before they moved out of Ebbets Field in Brooklyn. When I was a teenager in Hudson, we used to hear the Dodgers game being broadcast from Brooklyn on the radio. Red Barber, Vin's predecessor and mentor, was the Dodger broadcaster at that time. When attending the games, most everyone in the stands brought their transistor radio. It was as if we couldn't follow the game by just watching, without Vin Scully telling us what we were seeing! He soon won the hearts of his listeners. I was as much a fan of Vin, as I was of the Dodgers. I thought it would be great to have an opportunity to meet him some day. That day came in the spring of 1972, 14 years after the Dodgers arrived in our town; and, thereby, hangs this tale:*

Fig. 20 - "Vin" Scully in the Broadcast Booth at Dodger Stadium, L.A.

*One of the Directors of Edison Company, Mr. Terrell (Terry) Drinkwater (former CEO of Western Airlines) was a friend of Walter O'Malley, owner of the Los Angeles Dodgers. Occasionally, Vin Scully would join them for a golf game. Mr. Drinkwater knew that I was an avid Dodgers fan and a strong admirer of Vin Scully, as well. On one of these occasions he told Vin about my loyalty as a Dodgers fan, as well as my admiration for him. He noted my hope that I would get to meet him in person some day. Vin then wrote a letter to me delivered by Mr. Drinkwater. The letter read:*

"Dear Honor,

Our mutual friend, Terry Drinkwater, tells me that next to your loyalty to the Edison Company. you are an avid Dodgers fan. Please come to the broadcasting booth sometime during the season. I would like to say 'Hello.'

Warm wishes, Vin Scully"

*I was on "Cloud 9" and treasured that letter. I made copies to send to all of my family members.*

*When Len and I attended a Dodgers game early in the season, we went to the broadcasting booth during the third inning when Jerry Doggett (team member) was calling the game. I rang the bell and a staff member responded. I showed him the letter and he went inside with it. Vin Scully then came out, greeting us warmly, thanked me for my loyalty to the Dodgers and taking the time to come by and say "Hello." (Yes, he did hand his letter back to me.)*

*Vin Scully retired at the end of the 2016 season, after 67 years of broadcasting Dodgers baseball. The road which leads from Sunset Boulevard to the Dodgers stadium was renamed "Vin Scully Avenue."*

## Football

*Mr. Horton was a member of the Board of Trustees of the University of Southern California (USC). He was a graduate of Stanford University and his allegiance to his alma mater remained strong. As a Trustee, he was supportive of the USC football team, except when the opposing team was Stanford. As a Trustee he was entitled to tickets to any or all of the home games. Len and I* were offered his tickets occasionally, when he and his family did not use them. The seats were in a great location, and we enjoyed attending the games. This was during the years that O.J. Simpson was on the USC team and was their "hero."

Len's sister and brother -in -law (Marion and Lotie) sometimes joined us when we had the use of the tickets. Marion and Lotie were graduates of the University of California, Berkeley, and Len was a graduate of UCLA; thus, not supporters of USC, but rivals. I had to caution them to withhold their cheers or boos if their team was playinsg USC, as it would be inappropriate and embarrassing sitting in the midst of USC supporters.-

Mr. Horton offered us his tickets for one of the Rose Bowl games. It was the year that Pat Nixon, then First Lady, was Grand Marshall of the Rose Parade. She and her entourage were seated close to us in the "V.I.P" section. We were well aware of the Secret Service people seated around us. They changed their locations each quarter of the game.

# The Fifth Rung

## Success

# Chapter 20 – Corporate Secretary - September 20, 1979

Honor was the first female officer in the Southern California Edison Company. Hence, the title of this book.

**Southern California Edison Company**
P. O. BOX 800
2244 WALNUT GROVE AVENUE
ROSEMEAD, CALIFORNIA 91770

JACK K. HORTON
CHAIRMAN OF THE BOARD

TELEPHONE
213-572-2262

September 20, 1979

OFFICERS
DEPARTMENT HEADS
DIVISION VICE PRESIDENTS
DISTRICT MANAGERS
DIVISION MANAGERS & SUPERINTENDENTS

    Mr. J. C. Bobek, Secretary, has elected to retire effective November 1, 1979.

    As a result, the Board of Directors has elected Mrs. Honor Muller, currently Assistant Secretary, to the position of Secretary. Her election is to be effective November 1, 1979, at which time she will assume the responsibilities of that office and will report to Mr. H. Fred Christie.

    Mrs. Muller will continue to administer the secretarial affairs of my office in addition to assuming the responsibilities of Corporate Secretary.

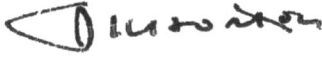

Fig. 21a - CEO's Letter to the Officers and Department Heads: Honor's Election - 1979

September 1979

From
Southern California
Edison Company

**SC EDISON DIRECTORS ELECT HONOR MULLER AS SECRETARY**

FOR IMMEDIATE RELEASE

ROSEMEAD, CA, Sept. 20--Honor Muller today was elected corporate secretary of Southern California Edison Company by the electric utility's board of directors, Jack K. Horton, board chairman and chief executive officer, announced.

Mrs. Muller succeeds Joseph C. Bobek, who will be retiring November 1 after more than 33 years of service with the Edison Company, the last four as corporate secretary.

Born and reared in Hudson, New York, Mrs. Muller started her business career with SCE in 1946. After working in various secretarial assignments in the company's power supply department, she took a year's leave of absence to complete a business course at Radcliffe College, Cambridge, Mass.

She rejoined Edison as a member of the executive officers' staff and became secretary to the president in 1959 and secretary to the chairman of the board in 1968.

On Dec. 21, 1978, Mrs. Muller was elected assistant secretary of the Edison Company.

She and her husband, Leonard, a retired SCE employee, reside in Los Angeles.

Fig. 21b - SCE Press Release

# News Release

Now that Honor has been promoted to Corporate Secretary, she is no longer just an Executive Assistant. Now that she is an Officer, she has overall responsibility of the Shareholder Services Department. She has the responsibiliy of recording all of the Board of Directors, Executive Committee, Board Committee and Officer's Council meetings, and, is the Custodian of the Corporate Seal. In addition, Mrs. Muller is responsible for the recording and certification of all official Southern California

Edison business, and in organizing the annual meeting of the SCE Stockholders.

When Honor became an Officer, she warranted a company car and her own parking space in the basement garage in the main building. The Company provided cars for all Officers. The CEO, President, and two senior Vice Presidents had assigned drivers. Drivers on standby had their own room in the garage. Parking spaces were allocated in the order of seniority level. The four most senior oficers were located close to the bank of elevators.

When Honor was elected Corporate Secretary there were 21 officers responsible for multiple divisions; all men. There is a hallway at the Corporate office in Rosemead with a gallery of photos of past CEOs mounted on the wall in the chronogical order of their service; again, all men. Today, women hold many of the high level positions at the officer level that were formerly held by men.

As Corporate Secretrary, Honor was also responsible for the operations of the Secretary's Department of 28 employees. This Department's function related to shareholder matters. This included issuance of dividends to shareholders, stock transfer, preparation and mailing of Annual Proxy Statements which accompanied the Annual Report to Shareholders. Honor's duties also included rccording the minutes of the monthly Board of Directors meetings, certain Board Committee meetings as well as the Annual Shareholders meeting

## The Southern California Edison Company

To give you an idea of the scope of the Southern California Edison Company size and operations let me start with what it does. *"One of the nations's largest investor owned utilities. It provides fourteen million people with electricity across a service territory of approximatelyy 50,000 square miles. The Service territory includes about 430 cities and communities with a total customer base of about 5 million residential and business accounts."* (Re: GOOGLE Profile on line)

Their General headquarters was located in downtown Los Angeles during the first 25 years of Honor's early employment with SCEC. In August of 1971, due to the need for more space, the headquarters moved out to Rosemead, California due east of the L.A. City limits.

As of December 31, 2017, Edison International and its consolidated subsidiaries had an aggregate of 12,521 full time employees. 12,234 of which were full time employees at SCE. Honor recalls that during her tenure there were about 14,000 employees. SCE has reduced its number of employees over the last 30 years despite its intervening growth.

Approximately 20% of power delivered to SCE's customers comes from utility-owned generation. In 2017 the sources of utility-owned generation were: 6% natural gas, 6% nuclear, 7% large hydroelectric, 1% small hydroelectric, and less than 1% solar sources. Wind and solar power generation percentage is growing. San Onefre and Palo Verde nuclear plants will be decommissioned by 2045 and 2046 respectively.

The power supply to customers is provided through distribution circuits. A circuit serves a given geographic area, and is given a name. There is a circuit named The Honor 16 KV Line out of Rosemead Substation.

In 1987, after Honor retired, SCE created Edison International. It was incorporated as a Holding Company of SCE, and as such has no operations of its own. Certain SCE Officers also serve on the staff of Edison International.

Fig. 22 - Southern California Edison Executive Officers as of 1984

Honor, the first and only female officer in The Edison Company (lower right).

**Southern California Edison Company**
P. O. BOX 800
2244 WALNUT GROVE AVENUE
ROSEMEAD, CALIFORNIA 91770

JACK K. HORTON
CHAIRMAN OF THE EXECUTIVE COMMITTEE

TELEPHONE
818-302-2262

February 11, 1985

Ms. Maura R. Walsh
Director of Financial Development
YWCA of Los Angeles
1125 W. 6th Street, Suite 400
Los Angeles, California 90017

Dear Ms. Walsh:

On behalf of the Southern California Edison Company I am honored to nominate Honor Muller, Corporate Secretary for Southern California Edison, for the 1985 Silver Achievement Award.

Mrs. Muller is one of the outstanding business women in Southern California. Honor is an example to all women in business of the results that can be achieved through leadership, hard work and dedication. Honor Muller takes risks in order to perform in an innovative and effective manner in the rapidly changing world of a utility with nuclear interests.

Mrs. Muller's dedication to professional and managerial development has been unequaled. She began her career with Edison in 1946 in an entry level secretarial position within the Power Supply Department. Her expertise and talents in business skills, insight in dealing with Edison business matters and in dealing with individuals has helped Mrs. Muller rise from her entry position to her current position as Corporate Secretary.

I trust sufficient information on Honor's outstanding qualities are included in the attached Nomination Form. If you should need additional details, please feel free to call me. It is with utmost respect that I endorse Mrs. Muller for this Award.

Sincerely,

Jack K. Horton
Chairman of the Executive Committee

Fig. 23 - CEO's Nomination of Honor for 1985 YWCA Silver Achievement Award

# Chapter 21 – Honor's Decision To Retire November 20, 1986

Honor Muller

**Southern California Edison Company**
P. O. BOX 800
2244 WALNUT GROVE AVENUE
ROSEMEAD, CALIFORNIA 91770

HONOR MULLER
SECRETARY

TELEPHONE
818-302-2802

November 20, 1986

MR. HOWARD P. ALLEN
CHAIRMAN OF THE BOARD AND
 CHIEF EXECUTIVE OFFICER

Because of my election to retire from active service, I hereby tender my resignation as Secretary of Southern California Edison Company to be effective as of the close of business on December 31, 1986.

Honor Muller

Fig. 24 - Honor's Letter of Resignation - November 20, 1986

RESOLUTION OF THE BOARD OF DIRECTORS OF
SOUTHERN CALIFORNIA EDISON COMPANY

Adopted November 20, 1986

RE: RESIGNATION OF CORPORATE SECRETARY
HONOR MULLER

WHEREAS, Mrs. Honor Muller has elected early retirement and has presented her written resignation as Corporate Secretary of this Company effective as of the close of business December 31, 1986; and

WHEREAS, this Board of Directors desires that the minutes of this corporation reflect an expression of sincere appreciation to Mrs. Muller for the many contributions she has made to the Company's advancement during her Edison career of more than 39 years; and

WHEREAS, Mrs. Muller's long and distinguished career began in 1946 when she joined Edison in the Power Supply Department. She held a number of increasingly responsible secretarial assignments in both the Power Supply and Executive Departments until 1957 when she took a leave of absence to pursue a Harvard-Radcliffe program in Business Administration; and

WHEREAS, after returning from this business program, Mrs. Muller rejoined the Company as a member of the Executive Officers' Staff. She served as Secretary to the President,

Fig. 25 – Board of Directors Acknowledgment Resolution - Page 1 of 2

Secretary to the Chairman of the Board and Assistant Corporate Secretary before her election to her present position of Corporate Secretary in 1979 which made her the first female corporate officer in the history of the Company; and

WHEREAS, Mrs. Muller, while serving as Corporate Secretary, has provided the leadership, farsightedness, and untiring dedication which has allowed her department to flourish and thereby provide continuing improvement in its service to the Company's shareholders; and

WHEREAS, in addition to the dedicated service she has provided to the Company, Mrs. Muller has given generously of her time and leadership ability through her involvement with numerous important business and professional associations. These include the American Society of Corporate Secretaries, the Stock Transfer Association, the Western Stock Transfer Association, and the Pacific Coast Electrical Association.

NOW, THEREFORE, BE IT RESOLVED, that the resignation of Honor Muller, our longtime friend and associate, be accepted with regret and that this Board of Directors hereby expresses to her its gratitude, respect and best wishes for the future.

Fig. 25 – Letter, Board of Directors' Resolution - Page 2 of 2

# HONOR MULLER
## Is Retiring After 39 Years With Edison!

If you would like to say goodbye
and wish Honor the best in her retirement,
there will be an open house held on
Wednesday, November 26
in the Employee Lounge from 2:00 p.m. to 4:00 p.m.

Scroll sheets (attached) to be returned to Vivian Monroy,
Room 240, G.O.1 by November 17, 1986.

Fig. 26 – Invitation to Honor's Retirement Party

## Honor's Retirement Parties

Lisa-Mickey-Lil-Bob-Len-Honor-Mally-Jeanne Moore-Milt

Fig. 27a - Honor's Retirement Party with Family– November 13, 1986

Jack and Betty Horton's retirement dinner party for Honor at the California Club November 24, 1986

Fig. 27b – Honor and Jack Horton

# Chapter 22 – Being Retired with Len

## RETIREMENT

Fig. 27c - Honor and Len in Retirement

You are "retired!" You spent the first 20% of your life growing up and schooling yourself to be a Secretary so that you could go out into the world on your own. You found the ideal employment situation, it met your range of talents. You spent the next 45% of your life applying all the considerable mental talents that you possessed, your courage and your ambition to seek out advanced business education, and most of all, your exemplary good, likable, moral character. That combination of all your life's experiences to date resulted in the final achievement of your working career, your election to be the Corporate Secretary of a major business institution and the first female officer employed by the Southern California Edison Company.

The Edison Company provides a generous Retirement Plan that includes a pension. Pension plans are being dropped by some large businesses these days. At SCEC, *"Employees hired before December 31, 2017 who are retiring after 10 years of service at or after age 55 with at least 10 years of service may be eligible for post-retirement medical, dental and vision benefits depending on a number of factors , including the employee's years of service, age, hire date and retirement date."* ( SCE International and Southern California Edison 2017 Annual Report.)

You've retired from business, but you haven't retired from life. Life goes on, things happen, Despite all the new freedom, you have to keep busy and there are places to go. You will find that there's never enough time in the day to take care of all you have to do.

# Chapter 23 – Honor's Letter To Vice President Bush
# Milt Had Died, February 26, 1987

WHEN GEORGE H.W. was Vice President, Milt was invited to a reunion of their fighter squadron aboard the retired *San Jacinto* aircraft carrier. When the war ended, he went into the insurance business and rose to the position of Vice President of the company. Sadly, Milt had lung cancer, but was in remission at the time of the Squadron reunion. He succumed of the disease on his 63rd birthday. He was the first of the seven Moore siblings to die.

Fig. 28 - Milton (Milt) Moore - V. P. George H.W. Bush with Milt - Page 1 of 3

C O P Y

March 1, 1987

The Honorable Vice President and Mrs. George H. Bush
Vice President's House
Washington, D. C. 20501

Dear George and Barbara:

This is the "harbinger" of sad news. My brother, Milt Moore, died Thursday evening, February 26, on his 63rd birthday.

As I think you knew, he was battling another tough round when he learned last fall that the cancer had attacked his spinal column. Your telephone call to Milt at that time, expressing your love and prayer support, was so meaningful to him. It provided a great lift and the warmth of your long friendship meant so much to Milt.

We have often expressed how thankful we were that Milt and Jeanne were able to attend your "40th Anniversary" celebration in Virginia in September 1984. It was a highlight in his life and the best thing that happened for him since his battle with cancer commenced in February 1984. He got a lot of mileage out of the memory of participating in that special event honoring you.

Milt leaves to us, his family, a marvelous legacy. His example of courage and positive attitide in dealing with such a difficult situation will always be a source of strength to each of us in facing any adversity in our lives. We are grateful that Milt is now free of any further problems, but it leaves a tremendous void in our lives, and, of course, we will miss him very much. I am also very thankful to God that Milt conquered his problem with alcohol -- he would have celebrated his 15th "AA Birthday" this month. He was very proud of that and rightly so. I thank the Lord that He let Milt become a whole person again and go on to be a source of help to so many others.

Fig. 29a - Honor's Letter to Vice President Bush – Page 2 of 3

- 2 -

    You are very much in our thoughts and prayers as we are so publicly aware of the problems you are dealing with in this difficult time for our nation. We appreciate your leadership role and want you to know that you have our support now and will continue to have it in the months ahead. We are pulling for you.

    With my loving wishes to both of you,

(Honor)

P.S. I retired as Corporate Secretary of Southern California Edison Company on January 1, after 39 years of service. I know you are acquainted with Jack Horton, Howard Allen, and others at SCE, and know what a fine organization it is. I was so pleased that you participated in the videotape presentation to our Citizenship Responsibility Group (CRG). It came off so well, and I was very proud. I had told Milt about it, and, of course, he was delighted to know about that.

Fig. 29b - Honor's Letter to Vice President Bush - Page 3 of 3

THE VICE PRESIDENT
WASHINGTON

March 27, 1987

Mrs. Leonard Frederick Muller
2648 Green Oak Place
Los Angeles, California  90068

Dear Honor:

    Thanks for your wonderful letter of March 1. Right after Milt died, I called Jeanne to tell her how sorry Barbara and I were.

    You know, Honor, that Milt was one of my closest friends. Even though we were separated by a continent and hadn't seen each other for years, the friendship remained strong. The minute I saw him at that 40th reunion on September 2, 1984, I knew he was still my close, dear friend. When he died, I felt a terrible wrench in my soul. I am sure it was nothing like the sense of loss that you feel and that Jeanne feels, but what I'm trying to say is that I loved him very much. I wish he were going to be around to help me next year -- if not in politics, just by giving me the strength that comes from one man loving another.

    Barbara sends her love.

Most sincerely,

Fig. 30 – V.P. Bush's Reply – March 27, 1987

Fig. 31 – V.P. George and Barbara Bush -Christmas - 1988

*After my retirement in January 1987, we sold the Del Mar Woods "townhouse" and concentrated on seeking out a more perfect location for our new life as retirees. We made a trip to the Northwest, visiting friends who had retired from Edison and relocated to* **Bellingham, Washington**. *They had a beautiful home overlooking Bellingham Bay. It was October and the weather was perfect. We decided we would give it a try and we purchased a home under construction just two doors away from our friends. We moved in May, 1989.*

*We found the weather factor, as well as the long distance from family and long-time friends in California, to be persuasive in our decision to sell and return to a more benign climate.*

Fig. 32– Bellingham House - 1989 –1991

Fig. 33 – Honor and Mally and the View from Bellingham House

# Mally's 75th Birthday Party

*Lil, Mally, Mickey, and Honor*

Fig. 34 - Mally's 75th birthday. April 5, 1994, Fair Oaks, California

By this time in Honor's life, two of her four brothers had died; Milton (Milt), February 26, 1987 and Claude, October 21, 1995. Aubrey and Mahlon (Mally) were still living.

**Claude**, the eldest, returned to civilian life after WWII and settled in Millburn, New Jersey. Upon discharge from the Army he returned to the Rimback Laundry, a business where he had been employed before serving in the Army. This was where he had met his future wife, Florence Tricarico, some years earlier. He became a Route Manager for the laundry until he retired at age 69. They had one daughter, Margaret (Peggy).

**Aubrey** was the second son born October 29, 1912. He married Betty Young before the war October 12, 1940. They were divorced in 1966. He and Betty had two daughters, Sandra (Sandy) and Susan. Both daughters were married before the divorce. Aubrey then married Betty Dietel November 23, 1968. He worked in the Sales Division of Western Pipe and Steel in the Los Angeles area before and after the war. When he retired about 1987, they moved from Burbank to Redding, California. He died there March 9, 2000 at age 88.

**Mally,** the third brother, was born April 5, 1919. He married Sylvia Tarvid in June, 1943, the niece of a fellow officer. It was a "war-time marriage" of short duration and dissolved upon his homecoming. He married again in 1948 and divorced in 1962, no children. He was employed by Aero Jet General Corporation in Fair Oaks, California where he met and married Twila Roy. They had two daughters, Cynthia (Cindy) and Jennifer. He retired as Manager of Procurement in 1988, after 32 years. He died December 21, 1997 at age 78.

**Milt,** the youngest brother, married Emy Lou Gordon in 1948. They were married 19 years before her death. He then married Jeanne Bentley in 1968. After being discharged from the U.S. Navy, he was employed by Cosgrove Insurance Company. Cosgrove later merged with Transamerica, Inc., where he became a Department Manager, and maintained that position until his death on February 26, 1987—his 63rd birthday.

Note: Each of Honor's four brothers died of different forms of cancer.

Fig. 35– Honor at age 68 and Mickey at age 70 in 1996

Fig. 35a - Mahlon (Mally) Horatio Moore Jr.- April 5, 1919-December 21, 1997

## Retirement in Carmel – 1991

Len and Honor moved from Bellingham, Washington to Carmel, California in May, 1991. In 1992 they joined the Carmel Presbyterian Church where she continued to employ her secretarial skills. Honor was only 58 in 1987 when she retired from SCEC. One of the things we know is that you can retire from business, but you can't retire from life. Active people, at that age, may seek out a second career and retire again. People who are self-sufficient, and do not need to supplement their retirement income, find satisfaction in volunteering. Honor did just that (between travels abroad) from 1992 until March of 1998 when they transferred to the First Presbyterian Church of Monterey.

> *During the time when Len and I were members of Carmel Presbyterian Church, I served on the Board and Executive Committee of the "Yellow Brick Road Benefit Shop." We met once a month to review requests for financial support from a wide range of organizations on the Monterey Peninsula. Our focus was*

*to assist entities that did not come under the "umbrella" of United Way support. As corresponding Secretary it was my job to respond to each request, either enclosing a check in my letter of support, or, explaining why their organization did not fall in the range of our giving. Yellow Brick Road supported "Sober Grad Night" for every high school in our area, including neighboring Salinas.*

*When I sent the checks to the respective schools, I would invite their "student committee" to come and visit our shop to see how the funds were generated, allowing us to support their programs.*

*We were delighted that some of them visited and thanked us "in person" for supporting them. I also served as a volunteer at the shop. It continues to be very successful, thanks to the generous donations of clothing, household goods and furniture.*

*I also volunteered as a Docent at La Mirada for ten years during this period. La Mirada is an extension of the Monterey Museum of Art. It plays an interesting and significant role in California history. It was formerly the private residence of Frank Work and his wife, Zizi. The original four-room adobe was one of three original small adobe homes built in the early 1800's in the Monterey area, this one for Antonio Castro, a retired soldier. For the next hundred years it was occupied by members of the Castro family.*

*In the 1900's another prominent California family, headed by General John Fremont, occupied the adobe. Fremont was later elected to the U.S. Senate and moved his family to Washinton, D.C. In 1946, Frank Work became the owner of this house, which had been enlarged over the years. The Works traveled extensively, acquiring fine art and furnishings from around the world for their home. Frank Work, who had survived his wife, had bequeathed the home and its furnishings to the Monterey Museum of Art, a historical gift to be enjoyed by the community. Docent tours were established to assist the public in their viewing of this unique collection.*

# Chapter 24 – Widowhood - April 16, 1999

## Remembering Len

---

*A Service in Witness to the Resurrection in Memory of*

**Leonard Muller**

September 10, 1910 - April 16, 1999

April 22, 1999                Four o'clock in the Afternoon

First Presbyterian Church of Monterey

---

Fig. 36 – Len's Memorial Service Bulletin

*LEN HAD BEEN blessed with very good health and a high level of energy throughout his life. We were planning a motor trip to New Mexico in early May, but two weeks before the scheduled trip, he was not feeling well. He described it as "Not hitting on all cylinders." He was admitted to the Emergency Room at the Community Hospital, where he was given a CT-Scan. During the Scan he had a brain stem stroke. The neurosurgeon told me the options; they could do what was termed a "clot buster" procedure, which may, or may not be successful. There was a possibility that he may not survive the procedure. If nothing was done, he probably would not survive. Although he survived the surgery, the damage from the stroke was too severe for recovery. During the next two days, his situation deteriorated dramatically, with no indication of improvement.*

*His son, Brian, flew from Washington, D.C., immediately. His sister Marion, came from San Diego. Mickey, my sister (and my "Gibraltar" on a human level), also came immediately to support me. They all had a chance to spend time with Len, although they were not certain that he was aware of their presence. He died in the late afternoon on Friday, April 16, 1999, at CHOMP (Community Hospital of the Monterey Peninsula) after only three days of being hospitalzed. April 16 was the birthday of my sisters, Lillian (Lil) and Margaret (Mickey). My birthday was only two days later on April 18.*

*Senior Pastor, Jay Bartow, First Presbyterian Church of Monterey, was a stong support throughout this period, as well as Associate Pastors, Sarah and Dwight Naves. Although Len and I had been members of "First Presbyterian" for only a year, the "Church family" surrounded me with love and caring. and provided food and loving condolences, followed with consoling visits by my closest friends.*

Life as a widow meant learning to live alone and adjust to her new life without a mate. She had many good friends who invited her to join them for lunch or dinner. She was financially secure, self reliant, and remains in excellent health, both physically fit and mentally sharp. She kept busy. She continued to be active in church activities such as; choir, Finance Committee, Bible study classes and later became a Deacon.

She enjoyed reading and shared that passion with her sister Mickey. Fortunately, she was able to drive and made a trip to Santa Barbara about every five weeks to visit Mickey. Lil and Bob Rufi, ( her other sister and her brother -in-law) lived in Pismo Beach. This was a convenient stop on the way to Santa Barbara from Carmel for a visit with them as well. Many of her friends expressed concern about Honor making such a long drive alone. She is a good driver and felt quite comfortable about undertaking a familiar drive.

She was fortunate to be able to remain in her own home. She was familiar with their financial situation and able to make the transition to being the person to pay the bills, to reconcile bank statements, etc. Her experience in the business world stood her in good stead. Among her many duties as Corporate Secretary, she had been responsible for recording the minutes of the monthly Board of Director's meetings which exposed her to financial reports and discussions at many levels.

Although none of her family lived within a hundred miles of Carmel, she often told me that she felt "very blessed' to have so many good neighbors and local friends to support her during this difficult period of "adjustment."  Honor  and Len had been married thirty-five years. She was thirty-five when they married in February, 1964. When Len died in April, 1999, her two sisters, Lil and Mickey were both living. Now, as of 2015, Honor is the sole survivor of the seven Moore siblings.

## Chapter 25 – Charles – 2001

A TWO-YEAR PERIOD between the loss of a mate, before establishing a new companionship, seems to be a sociably and morally acceptable time span for the survivor to have healed from grieving and moved on to build a new life with another. In 2001, she added a companion to the mix, me.

Fig. 37 - Charles Franklin Hutchins, Lt. Colonel, U.S. Army, Retired

That's me. I'm Charles. I'm a widower. I live alone in a 4 bedroom, 3 bath house in Del Monte Beach , Monterey, California, 5 miles from Honor's house in Carmel. My house is one block, above the beach, overlooking Monterey Bay. I'm a retired Army Lieutenant Colonel, Army Aviator, published writer and businessman. I drive a Z-4 BMW Roadster when Honor is my passenger, and I own a BMW 525 Touring, utility type vehicle. that I use for every day transportation.

# My Nine Lives

Starting in 1927, I grew up in a small town in Michigan during The Great Depression. I was a:

**Singer** – I've been a singer all my life. In 1940, the family moved to Detroit where I was the "Frank Sinatra" of my high school; the girls screamed their heads off. I've been a soloist in weddings and concerts; sung in quartets, glee clubs, musicals, choral organizations and church choirs.

**Sailor** – when I graduated from high school, I enlisted in the regular navy for two years, where I was a fire-tugboat engineer at Pearl Harbor, 1946-47.
I sang in the Blue Jacket Choir in boot camp on Sundays, and at special off-base performances, like one in Chicago for Manufacturers' Association.
I walked around a turret ring on the sunken "Arizona."
I walked the deck of the raised "Oklahoma" before she sank on the way to Seattle.
We towed the radioactive "Nevada" into the harbor. We fought eight ship and dock fires.

**Actor** - I had lead roles in eight community theater plays and musical productions; four in Honolulu and four in Lansing, Michigan.

**Student** – when I was discharged from the Navy in 1947, I thought that I wanted to be in show business. I spent a month in New York, auditioning for a part in a Broadway show, until I had an attack of appendicitis.
I graduated, *cum laude*, from Michigan State, on the G.I. Bill, with a degree in music education; but I got called to active duty and decided I'd rather make a career out of the Army, than to teach in public school. Besides, I was a lousy piano player.

**Soldier** - I was commissioned from senior ROTC in the Armor Branch of the Army. I spent two years in tanks at Fort Hood. During my military career, I commanded units at all levels from tank platoon to combat aviation battalion. One of the four companies that I commanded was at Fort Knox. My company provided the Fort Knox Honor Guard, for visiting foreign dignitaries.

**Aviator** – I earned my wings in 1954. I spent the next 20 years flying airplanes and helicopters; first in Germany, patrolling the *iron curtain* in a Cessna fixed wing from 1955 to 1958.
I accepted a Regular Army commission in 1957. Then, a year in Korea in 1961-62, near the DMZ. Next, helicopter school and *Command and General*

*Staff College.* Then, back to Germany as commander of *the Aviation Company, 3rd Armored Cavalry Regiment* during 1966, until it was my turn to go to Vietnam.

In 1967, I organized and trained a recon airplane company of 24 Cessna "Bird Dogs" at Fort Hood, Texas and took it to "the Delta" in Vietnam for a year. The last 8 months there, as a Lt Colonel, I commanded the 307th Combat Aviation Battalion. I had my own UH1D " Huey" helicopter and crew. I flew at 700 feet almost daily for 700 hours, and sustained only one hit. From there I was assigned to *Combat Developments Experimentation Command* at Fort Ord, California. I planned helicopter gun-ship tactics experiments for seven years, as aviation project officer. I retired in 1975.

**Merchant** – for the next 28 years, starting in 1974, my wife and I, and our 5 children, ran 3 Christmas shops; in Carmel-by-the-Sea, The Crossroads and in The Barnyard, until 2002 when I retired-retired.

My wife, Janet, died in 1999. We closed the business in 2002. My children, all found higher paying jobs.

**Writer** – then, as a widower for two years, I wrote five books, one published, and I'm working on this sixth one with my friend of 18 years, Honor Muller; it's her story.

**Retiree** - I retired from the Army in 1975, with 25 years service, and 28 in the retail business, until 2002. In 2001, I had joined the Presbyterian Church. I sing in the choir. My friend, Honor and I date. We eat out three times a week and we watch three *Netflix* DVD movies each week.

I now have five married children, seven grand-children, and ten great-grand children.

My wife had died three months after Len had died in 1999. Two years later I joined my church and the choir. I served three years as a Deacon and a year as an Elder. Meeting Honor introduced me to a whole new wonderful way of life.

I entered Honor's life when I joined the church choir in 2001. Honor was a member of the choir. We started dating when we were set up by Gita Blair. Gita was the "Mother of the choir" and very active in music circles. She and retired Army Colonel, Larry Blair, had season tickets for the Monterey Symphony concerts. They were friends of the conductor. The Blairs were Symphony supporters. The Mayor of Monterey and a City Council member are members of our First Presbyterian Church of Monterey. The Mayor's wife is a soprano soloist in the choir. Honor is an alto. I am a baritone. Singing is just another element we share in common in our lives.

Honor's version of how we met:

*After Len's death in April, 1999, I joined The Chancel Choir of the First Presbyterian Church of Monterey, at the urging of Linda Foy, a choir member, and a dear and loving friend. She knew that it was difficult to find myself sitting alone in the Congregation. Linda had been in the choir for some time and assured me that the choir was a close-knit and caring group, an extension of family. I found that she was right. I felt the warmth and support of this group immediately. Becoming a member of the choir was one of the most important moves I could have made.*

*About two years later, Charles Hutchins, a baritone, joined. I learned that he had become a widower just a few months after I became a widow. We had many cordial and friendly conversations at our social gatherings. Gita and Larry Blair, two very special people in the choir, arranged to "Set us up." We were both invited to lunch at their Monterey Country Club after church service on Sunday (We were not told that the other was also a guest.) until Gita suggested that we carpool -Honor riding with Charles. Charles had a better idea. He followed me home so that I could leave my car. I rode to the Country Club with him.*

*Following a delightful luncheon, that included Gita's cousin and her husband, visiting from Philadelphia, and Arthur and Mary Ellen Reedie. Mary Ellen was our Choir Director at that time. Charles drove me home. When he first saw where I lived, he commented that he and his wife, Jan, had looked at this property when it was being built. I invited him to come in and see the finished product. This offered us a fine opportunity for "Getting to Know You." Four hours later, he left, (Impressed with how much we had in common.) He invited me to join him for the upcoming "Camerata Singers" concert." When we had a parting hug and kiss, he said he would be in touch about the Concert. He telephoned the next day and invited me to dinner that Wednesday and I accepted.*

*It happened to be Valentine's Day - a romantic "Anniversary" date. Now, sixteen years later, the romance continues, and Charles is stlll my "Boyfriend."*

I had been in that house in 1991, when it was new - Serendipity! We had a lot in common having lived a similar life through the Great Depression, WWII and successful careers. I was born in September in 1927 and she was born in April 1928.

I dropped my search for a widow who would consider marriage when I dated Honor on Valentines Day 2001. We've been dating ever since.

Fig. 38 - Honor with Charles

Fig. 39 - Honor At Home

# Chapter 26 – Corresponding With President George H.W. Bush - 2009

124 Sea Foam Avenue<br>
Monterey, CA 93940<br>
March 10, 2009

Dear President Bush,

I just finished reading your autobiography, *"LOOKING FORWARD"*, and James Bradley's, *"FLYBOYS."* I know how devoted you are to your Squadron mates. I'm referring to MILTON MOORE who flew a diversion pattern while you were being picked up by the *Finback*.

I was told by his sister, Honor Moore Muller, that he was a member of your wedding party. I note that you confirmed that on page 41 of your book. As I believe you know, Milt died of cancer, February 26, 1987, twenty-two years ago on his $63^{rd}$ birthday. Honor tells me that she received a warm message of condolences from you.

I think you and Barbara might be interested in knowing that of the seven children in the Moore family, two sisters, Margaret and Honor, have survived. Honor is the younger, and with the death of our spouses in 1999, we have become close friends. Honor retired from Southern California Edison where she was the Corporate Secretary, the first elected female officer in that Company. She knows all the details about your experience at Chichi Jima and takes pride in the fact that her brother, Milt Moore, was a Naval Aviator and a mate of yours on the *San Jacinto*.

Her claim to fame is the fact that your son, our $43^{rd}$ President, slept in her bed when you and Barbara visited the Moore family. Young George was about two years old at the time. Honor recalls that during your visit, George was put down for a nap in the bedroom that she and her Sister Margaret shared. While the adults were visiting, George came out of the bedroom, whimpering softly. Barbara took him on her lap, listening to what he was whispering in her ear. She comforted him saying, "Yes, George, I know you are in a strange bed, but you need your nap, so you must be very brave." Barbara then took him back to the bedroom to resume his nap. Honor is fond of telling that story whenever the opportunity arises, preceded by saying, "President Bush slept in my bed!"

I retired from the Army in 1975 as a Lt. Col. after twenty-five years of military service. Twenty years of that service was in Army Aviation. I commanded a Combat Aviation Battalion in the Delta in Vietnam during 1967-68 at the height of the war through "TET". I share your love of flying; But, I don't think I would have the courage to jump out of a perfectly good airplane, as you have done in recent years, when you didn't have to jump!

Both Honor and I have great respect and fondness for both you and Barbara. I agreed with every step you took in office, and as loyal Republicans, we supported George 43 in every decision he made.

Fig. 40a - Charles Letter To President George H.W. Bush -March, 2009 - Page 1 of 2

Bradley wrote that only five of the original fourteen members of your Squadron survived the war. I assume Milt Moore was one of that number. I thought you would like to know that Milt's surviving family members are well, and that they hold you in high regard. Your friendship with Milt means a great deal to them.

We are grateful that Barbara's heart surgery went well. With her, "We must be brave," outlook on life, we know that she is taking it in her stride.

Respectfully,

CHARLES F. HUTCHINS
LTC USA RET

Honor's address:
Honor Muller
3594 Eastfield Court
Carmel, CA 93923

Fig. 40b - Charles Letter to President George H,W, Bush-March 2009 - Page 2 of 2

In 2009 I had been reading George Bush's account of the downing of his aircraft. It occurred to me that he might be interested in knowing that his friend, Milt Moore, had two surviving sisters. I sent my letter to his Library address in Houston, Texas, where he had his office in retirement. To my surprise and pleasure, he wrote back and sent two copies of his latest book on his war experience, *George Bush - His WWII War Years*; one for me and one for Honor.

GEORGE BUSH

May 5, 2009

Dear Charles,

Please forgive the delay in acknowledging your thoughtful letter of March 10 about Milt Moore.

Milt was, indeed, my great and good friend. We shared a lot of happy times together, and a lot of sad times, too. I cried when he died. He was a wonderful person and a special friend to me.

I thought you and Honor might like to have copies of a book about my Navy days by Robert Stinnett. There are quite a few references to Milt in the book.

Thanks again for writing. Please pass along to Honor my very best wishes.

Sincerely,

G Bh

Lieutenant Colonel Charles F. Hutchins
USA (Retired)
124 Sea Foam Avenue
Monterey, CA 93940

Fig. 41 - President Bush's Reply.- May, 2009

May 30, 2009

President George H. W. Bush
George Bush Presidential Library and Museum
1000 George Bush Drive West
College Station, Texas 77845

Dear George:

     Your warm and thoughtful response to Charles Hutchins' recent letter to you was a delight to both Charles and me. Thank you so much for your wonderful letter and the signed copies of Robert Stinnett's book covering your World War II days as a naval aviator. The many references to my brother Milt Moore are indeed heart warming to me. This book is a treasure, and I do appreciate your thoughtfulness so much. As expected, my friend Charles is digesting it word for word, telephoning me occasionally to direct my attention to certain sections of the book.

     I am always pleased to see you and Barbara on television from time to time. It is good to know that your life is "CAVU."

     With my affectionate wishes to you and Barbara,

                                            Honor Muller
                                            3594 Eastfield Court
                                            Carmel, CA 93923

Fig. 42 - Honor's "Thank You" Letter to President Bush

# Chapter 27 – Remembering Lil and Bob-2002

THEY HAD NO children together. Bob had a son and a daughter from a previous marriage.

Lil had a stroke on December 28, 1983. She was able to remain in their home until 2001, when she needed more care than Bob could handle. She had to be admitted to a nursing care facility very close to their home. Bob faithfully visited her twice a day until she died April 14, 2002, two days before her 86th birthday. They had been married 31 years.

Fig. 43 - Lillian (Lil) Moore Rufi and Robert (Bob) Glenn Rufi

Bob Rufi died one month later, May 13, 2002. They were both cremated and buried in the Los Osos Valley Memorial Park in Los Osos, California. Just as the burial ceremony for Bob was to begin, I noticed a Marine firing squad attending a nearby ceremony. I thought that since Bob was a War Veteran, he was entitled to a Gun Salute. I approached the Colonel in charge of the detail; he was more than willing to set up and provide the appropriate send-off. I learned later that he had already agreed to have his team perform. I didn't have to use my own "pull," as an Army Lt. Colonel, to see that Bob was honored in this way.

Fig. 44 – Honor's Home, since 1991, and her new 2014 Mercedes In Carmel, California

# Chapter 28 – Remembering Margaret

Fig. 45 - Margaret (Mickey) Lois Moore holding "Maisie"

MARGARET DIED AT 3:45 p.m., May 25, 2015, at Serenity House in Santa Barbara, California, after a series of four strokes, starting November 4, 2014, with bleeding in the brain. She had just returned home from marketing when she lost consciosness and fell in her driveway. She was found the next morning by the Newspaper carrier.

She and Honor had retuned home just a few days earlier from a vacation trip to Mendocino. She survived that episode for several weeks. Her doctor ascribed her survival to the fact that she had been exposed to chilly overnight weather causing hypothermia keeping the brain from swelling. Sadly, the strokes reoccured 3 times, a few weeks apart; each time she seemed to have been stabilized and was discharged from the hospital to a rehabilitation facility.

She is survived by her daughter, Lisa Cervantes, and her son, Spencer Evan Nilson, four granddaughters and one great granddaughter. Honor, her younger sister, is now the last member of the Moore family.

Following her funeral service at her church in Montecito, Mickey's ashes were scattered off the coast of Santa Barbara by her son, on his surf board, as she had requested.

Fig. 46 - Mickey's son, Spencer Nilson,
delivering Mickey's ashes
to the wind and sea

# Chapter 29 – The Last Moore

*Claude – Honor – Mally – Mickey – Milt – Lil – Aubrey*

Fig. 47 - The Seven Moore siblings At Milt's house In Glendale, CA - 1984

HONOR IS THE ONLY member of the Mahlon and Henrietta Moore family still alive. All four brothers died of cancer, each from a different type of cancer. She is the youngest of their seven children; born into a family of the "Greatest Generation" of the 20th Century. She has been blessed with good health and a good level of energy. This allows her to actively participate in volunteering, as well as enjoying an active social life. Many times she is an early arrival at social gatherings and the last to leave. Her family and friends are in awe of her phenomenal memory. Her family has told me that when they cannot recall details of a family event, or someone's birthday, they know they can always call Honor. Her caring nature is evident in her relationship with family and friends. Her generosity benefits her family, her church and many charitable causes. We have much in common and find that we agree on many issues concerning religion and politics which makes for a compatible relationship.

At this writing, starting in 2016, Charles was 88, and Honor was 87, enjoyimg good health. She never said,"Yes." The offer is still on the table. (They have been "dating" 19 years.)

# Chapter 30 – Role Model

HONOR'S SECRET TO success is a matter of moral character, intelligence, loyalty, caring, generosity, ambition, and exceptional memory; all of which she possesses in abundance. She was driven to excel. She took advantage of opportunities as they were revealed She is a role model for young ladies who are at the crossroads of life. She is proof of the fact that wealth is not, necessarily, a prerequisite to achieving success. In other words, if she can achieve success out of humble beginnings, you can, too.

She was brought up in a Christian community in the days when doors of the church and home were not kept locked. Hobos in search of employment were fed by mother at the back door. Being a Christian provided the foundation of her charitable, caring nature throughout her life. She loves people and dogs, and they love her.

Her loyalty extends to her co-workers and friends. For example, she writes over 100 Christmas cards. She is constantly on the telephone with her myriad of family and friends. Her memory is legendary among those who know her. She remembers your name, your birthday, your anniversary, your wedding day, the names of your children and their birthdays and she sends each one a caring card. She is a marvel. All this caring is reciprocated. Everyone in her circles knows, loves and respects her.

Her intelligence is best revealed by her phenomenal memory which stood her in such high regard by her superiors.

Here is what the CEO of Southern California Edison Company thought of her; (An extract of his letter of recommendation, to The L.A. YWCA, of Honor for their 1985 Achievement Award.)

*"Mrs. Muller has an extraordinary ability to deal fairly and effectively with individuals at all levels from Company Directors to entry-level employees. Honor Muller has that indefinable quality possessed by people who ultimately achieve leadership roles, regardless of walk of life. It is an attribute that encompasses an ability to retain moral values; a need to attain excellence in their profession; a willngness to take risks in order to be innovative and continue growing; an ability to not lose sight of the "big picture" while working on the more narrow,*

*immediate one; over-laid wih a humanism that permeates and gives dignity to everything they do.*

*In Honor, this quality takes form in her quiet dignity which is evident to everyone who comes in contact with her. Her excellent skills allowed her to immediately gain the confidence of those with whom she worked when she started with the Company in 1946, in an entry position as stenographer.*

*While working as a secretary to the Chairman of the Board, she decided to take a"job-risk" in order to sharpen her already acute skills and business acumen and applied for a year's leave-of-absence to enroll in the Harvard/Radcliff Graduate Program in Business Administration in Cambridge, Massachusetts. The "risk"paid off, and upon her return she was assigned to the new President of Southern California Edison, Mr. Jack Horton, who was hired to that position from an outside organization. Honor's extensive Company background, facilitated by her newly acquired skills, contributed tto the effectiveness of Mr.Horton in his new position. Honor and Mr. Horton worked as an effective team. Then, in 1979, her abilities were given full recognition and she was elected Corporate Secretary. She became the first woman Corporate Officer of Southern California Edison Company.*

*(S) Jack K. Horton*
*Chairman of the Executive Committee*

# Epilogue

Now in retirement, Honor is self-sufficient. She owns a home in a gated community and is secure with a company pension annuity and adequate health care coverage. She has an active social life through her church activities, including singing in the choir, attending Bible study classes, as well as enjoying the company of her many friends.

If you are a single young lady about to enter the job market, the "Glass Ceiling" has been shattered. Today, many high level positions in major companies are filled by women who may owe their place in the work force to pioneers such as Honor Moore Muller.

Fig. 48 - Charles and Honor Celebrating the New Year, 2016, at their favorite upscale "Watering Hole," Anton and Michel, in Carmel- by-the-Sea, California.

Here's to you, dear reader, you made it! Here's a Toast to you for your fortitude in finishing Honor's story. Our goal was to describe what one young lady starting out in the business world was able to accomplish; how she did it and what events and environment influenced her rise "Through The Glass Ceiling." Perhaps reading about Honor's success might inspire some other young lady to carry the torch, and to know that because of pioneers like Honor that they too can succeed in business. We hope that it was "A Good Read" for you. "CHEERS!"

**THE END**

www.ingramcontent.com/pod-product-compliance
Lightning Source LLC
Chambersburg PA
CBHW041507220426
43661CB00017B/1276